Beaded Tassels, Braids & Fringes

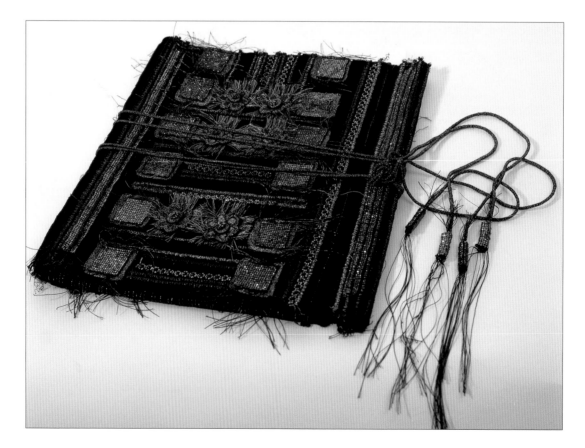

Beaded book cover combining machine embroidery with flower chains,
strips and squares of beading, and blackberries.

Beaded Tassels, Braids & Fringes

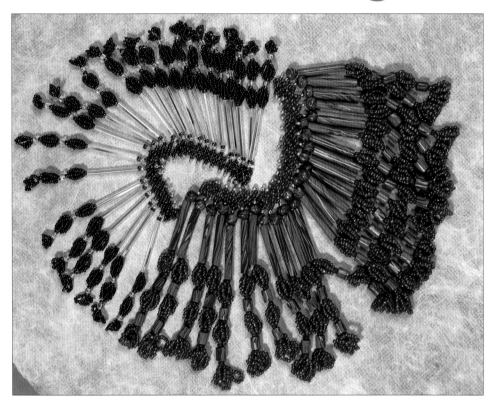

Valerie Campbell-Harding

Sterling Publishing Co., Inc.
New York

Library of Congress Cataloging-in-Publication Data
Campbell-Harding, Valerie.
    Beaded tassels, braids & fringes / Valerie Campbell-Harding.
        p.   cm.
    Includes index.
    ISBN 0-8069-4891-4
    1. Beadwork. 2. Tassels. I. Title.
  TT860.C36   1998   98-46795
  745.58'2—dc21   CIP

10 9 8 7 6 5 4 3 2 1

Published by Sterling Publishing Company, Inc.
387 Park Avenue South, New York, N.Y. 10016

© 1999 by Valerie Campbell-Harding

Distributed in Canada by Sterling Publishing c/o Canadian Manda Group,
One Atlantic Avenue, Suite 105, Toronto, Ontario, Canada M6K 3E7

Distributed in Great Britain and Europe by Cassell PLC Wellington House,
125 Strand, London WC2R 0BB, England

Distributed in Australia by Capricorn Link (Australia) Pty Ltd. P.O. Box 6651,
Baulkham Hills, Business Centre, NSW 2153, Australia

Printed in Hong Kong
All rights reserved

Sterling ISBN 0-8069-4891-4

Acknowledgments

Many thanks to my colleagues Lynn Horniblow and Ann Mockford for passing on some methods and techniques I had not known before and for allowing me to photograph many of their tassels for this book. Also thanks to the students who developed my ideas during courses and allowed me to photograph their tassels.

Peter Read B.Sc., LRPS, took all the photographs in his studio, made many suggestions for displaying the tassels and fringes, and did reshoots with unfailing good humor.

You might be interested in the software used for the diagrams. I work on a Power Macintosh and used Canvas 5 for most diagrams, Stitch Painter Gold with the beading module for the charts, and Photoshop 4 where necessary.

CONTENTS

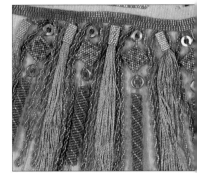
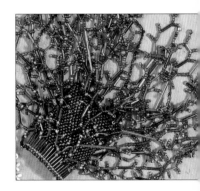

INTRODUCTION

Passementerie—French for "trimmings," and to my mind a much nicer word—covers the whole range of tassels, braids, cords, fringes, and buttons. In this book, I am concerned only with beaded passementerie, and you'll find here historical examples from the late nineteenth century and early twentieth. Think of the elegant beaded tassels designed by Erté or the wonderfully layered-fringe 1920s dresses.

Afghanistan is the only country which has historically made beaded cords and tassels in any quantity, and they are quite easy to find in most places. That is no reason why you cannot make your own tassels, however. But where can you use beaded tassels, braids, and fringes? Where not?

Tassels, braids, cords, and fringes make excellent finishing touches for clothing, bags, cushions, or simply to wear as jewelry. Larger tassels can be worn around your neck on a cord, and maybe tiny matching ones as earrings. A tassel can hang from a hat, a cupboard door latch, or on a light cord, or be used as a belt end or a bookmark. Tassels can decorate the corners of cushions, or hang from small bags or the lids of embroidered boxes. They can identify small things, like scissors or a pen, so that you can identify and quickly find your own.

Beaded fringes add much interest to the bottom of lampshades, glistening when the light is turned on. A fringe around the edge of a cushion, or hanging from a small evening bag, adds richness and color. In multiple rows, bead fringes can cover the front of a vest or small bag, adding the special weighted movement that is an aspect of rich beading.

Beaded cords or braids can trim cuffs, collars, seams and yokes of bags, cushions, jackets, and vests, or be used as hat bands. Some of them can be worn as bracelets, ankle bands, or around the neck. Also, I think of them as a decoration, as well as a finish, on embroidered book covers or picture frames.

I like to have tassels hanging all over the house—from curtain pulls and keys in wall cupboard doors to handles of corner cupboards. They dangle from light pulls, circle the necks of old brass oil lamps, shimmer from tall table lamps or wall lights. Anywhere that light catches the glints and emphasizes the color, tassels remind me that life is fun.

Some crystal and jet beaded tassels
from the 1920s and 1930s.

8

Small hard tassels to identify
your belongings, with painted
tassel molds decorated with
narrow braids.

9

BEADING BASICS

If you're a craftsperson, you may already have much of the equipment that you would need in order to do the beading in this book. If so, this first section could be used as a checklist, to see if there is anything new that you haven't yet heard about or anything you needed for other crafts and might want to have ready. If not, here are my shopping suggestions.

EQUIPMENT

Needles: I recommend that you use the best English beading needles; they are available anywhere. I use a size 10 most often, but you might need a finer one if the holes in your beads are on the small side. Some people suggest using fine short needles, such as sharps, for working peyote or brick stitches, but I like the long beading needles, as I find I can pick up the beads more easily. They tend to bend after a short time but, once you get the hang of it, this can actually be an advantage. You will also need a mattress needle, which is long enough to reach through the hole in the tassel mold to pull the cord through with a sling.

Thread: Beading thread needs to be strong enough not to break when you jerk it. I like Nymo thread, a specialist beading thread, because it is flat and goes through the long eye of a beading needle more easily. Other beading threads are round and you may need to flatten them with your teeth before they will go through the needle's eye. Use a darker color thread than your beads and it will look like a shadow—a paler thread shows up too much. You will also need button thread, or a fine strong linen thread, with which to stitch the skirts.

Beeswax: If the thread you are using continually knots, you can use beeswax or a silicon jelly to coat the thread and solve the problem. I don't usually bother.

Scissors: Use a small scissors for cutting the thread. If tiny ends still stick out above the beads, you can burn them off at any time with a flame.

Pliers: You will need long-nosed pliers, flat and ridged on the inside, to grab and pull your needle through tight places.

Velvet or chamois leather: I find a piece of velvet or chamois glued or laced to a piece of thick card about five or six inches square quite handy. Use a white one for most beads and a black one for pale colors. Spill out your beads onto this platform and you will find it much easier to pick them up. If the beads are in a dish or tin lid, you need to use a finger to scoop them onto the needle, which wastes time. I hold the needle parallel to the velvet board, and the beads just "tip" right onto it.

Lap tray: My lap tray has a large cushion underneath, filled with tiny polystyrene balls, so I can adjust its angle. When you are sitting on a sofa, a lap tray can keep the beads just where you want them and at a comfortable working level.

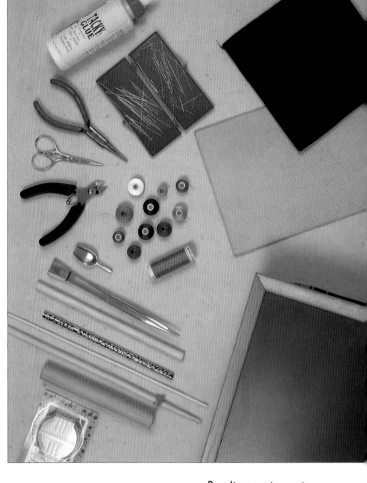

Beading equipment: needles, thread, pliers, scissors, glue, rods, velvet-covered card

Lighting: I find that having a floor lamp at the work area, with a donut-shaped fluorescent bulb surrounding a magnifying glass handy, is perfect for working with beads. I myself don't have need of a magnifying glass yet; but no doubt the time will come. Having a daylight bulb in the floor lamp removes some of the glare and makes it easier to choose the bead colors, whereas using a fluorescent bulb cuts down on the heat when doing close work.

Comb: If you can believe it, a dog comb is perfect for combing yarn skirts!

Cord winder: An actual winder is better for making cords than using a pencil and door handle. It's also much quicker. If you can't find one, you can also use a two-way drill and a cup hook.

Dowel rods: Gather a selection of dowels, chopsticks, round pencils, bamboo knitting needles and wooden skewers as "supports" for your beading.

Glues: I use thick, tacky PVA glue for rolling gimp, yarn, and beads onto wooden molds, and also for attaching beaded braids. You may prefer other glues, so just try them.

Wooden tassel molds: These molds are easier to find than they used to be, with wood turners now producing them in bulk for the crafts trade. You might persuade a wood turner you know to make a few or several for you. You can also substitute cardboard or plastic cylinders from the inside spools of thread or tape, drawer knobs (you'll need to drill holes through them), large wooden beads, or even small wooden candle holders or egg cups.

Skirt boards: These are usually made of wood, but you can make your own by gluing two strong pieces of stiff card together. Make two, measuring 5 by 7 inches and 6 by 8 inches, to start off with, then more as you need them.

YARNS

The best yarn to use for beaded tassels is fairly fine. Thick yarn looks clumsy with beads, and also tends to be uncontrollable. You should also consider what the cut ends look like, because they can split and separate. The kind of yarn fiber to use depends on the look you want: wool is springy and bouncy, cotton is heavy and a bit lanky, acrylic is fluffy, and so on. Metallic yarns are usually too stiff, and embroidery threads are too expensive. Silk is always the best...but it does cost a fortune.

My preference is a fine rayon, either twisted or spun (it looks like wool and sometimes comes mixed with a bit of acrylic). Chainette, fine-knitted tubing used for fringes and tassels, and folded twisted rayon yarns hang beautifully and never seem to get untidy or tangled. Buy these from weaving suppliers rather than at knitting shops. I always go for the finest Chainette I can find, and the 200/2 rayon; I recommend that you do, too. I have sometimes used unsuitable yarns for tassel skirts and then covered them with a vertical netting. It's a vast improvement, but such tassels still hang rather stiffly—without the "movement" that's so important to a tassel.

Yarns of rayon, silk, linen, and metallic fibers, and two tassels
made from mixing different fibers together.

BEADS

This tassel shows a gentle contrast between large and small, shiny, transparent and matte beads and wooden beads covered with fine thread.

When I first started using beads for embroidery, there weren't very many different colors or types available to choose from—although there were always plenty of different shapes and sizes. So crafters would spend time dyeing or painting beads; but we found that the color sometimes faded—was not always lightfast—which was disappointing. Now there are many different surface finishes and the color range is enormous. This is absolutely wonderful in theory, but it makes your choice extremely difficult. If you're like me, when you cannot decide which one to have, you buy both! Then, of course, you have the further problem of storing them and in such a way that you can easily and quickly find the color you want when you want it.

TYPES OF BEADS

Small beads are nearly always made of glass, and it is the amount of transparency and the surface finish that give them character. Very small round beads are called rocailles, or seed beads. Seed beads come from the Czech Republic and Slovakia (previously called Czechoslovakia), India, France, China (their bead shapes can run from somewhat to very uneven), or from Japan (which produces the most even seed beads). The Japanese currently supply 80 percent of the world market and are continually producing different shapes and finishes.

When you buy beads, a reputable supplier will provide information in the catalog and tell you, on the bead packet, what type of bead it contains and the kind of surface finish it has. This is a good way to learn the different kinds of beads available.

BASIC BEAD FINISHES

You'll find that most small beads will fall into the following groups:
❖ Transparent—clear colors that allow the light to shine through. These have a wider range of color, so are easier to blend from one shade to another. Since

A variety of surface finishes available today: shiny, matte, opaque, transparent.

the thread, however, shows through, thread color may affect the bead color.

❖ Opaque—solid-color beads that you cannot see through. The colors are therefore stronger, but the range of available colors is limited. These beads can be etched to make them matte.

❖ Color transparent and lined—"see-through" colored beading with a hole color different from that of bead; for example, a purple bead with pink lining.

❖ Color-lined transparent—clear beads with a colored lining. The color from a lining is more durable than with surface-painted beads.

❖ Silver-lined—transparent beads lined inside with silver. They are brilliant—"glitzy." Also, bleaching removes the silver lining, often leaving subtle coloring you just can't buy.

❖ Gold- or copper-lined transparent or milky beads.

❖ Greasy—the beads transmit light, but you cannot actually see through them.

❖ Opal—a murky, milky, or translucent bead.

❖ Satin—beads with a satiny look and color that varies based on viewing angle.

❖ White-hearts—beads having an inner core of white glass.

ADDED FINISH

An extra finish is often added to beads. These fall into the following groups:

❖ Iris, AB (Aurora Borealis) or iridescent—coated with metal salts that are burned off. These beads resemble an oil slick or a rainbow—different colors together on each bead.

❖ Luster—a vari-colored finish on any type of bead.

❖ Pearl—used to describe luster beads.

❖ Matte or frosted—velvety beads that are dipped in acid or tumbled to give them a completely matte surface. They can be single- or multi-colored and are wonderful when contrasted with shiny or metallic beads. They are easy to see when you are beading. You can matte your own by using an etching fluid.

❖ Ceylon—a pearled finish.

❖ Metallic—glass beads with a metal-like coating, not necessarily permanent: the very bright colors are suspect.

❖ Metallic iridescent—pretty and permanent.

❖ Matte metallic—metallic beads with a matte finish.

BEAD SHAPES

Most seed beads are round; but they may often be longer than wide, which means that the number of beads in a row measures differently in rows worked. Most of the beads used in this book fall into the following groups:

❖ Round—many sizes (8 to 24), seed or rocailles; pony beads are larger and give added weight to the ends of fringes.

❖ Two-cuts—chopped glass tubes, like very short bugles; these beads can cut thread.

❖ Three-cuts—small irregular facets over the whole bead; they often come in irregular sizes.

❖ Bugles—tubes 02–99 mm, plain or twisted, often with sharp ends that can cut threads. The Japanese bugles are better finished.

❖ Miyuke Delica or Toho—these Japanese beads are tiny cylinders with very large holes, but they are the most regular. They look like little tiles, or the segments of a butterfly wing, when seen through a microscope. Wonderful alone, they are difficult to use combined with other beads in loom work or the peyote or brick stitches because of the different shape.

❖ Hex cuts—tiny tubes that have a hexagonal cross section rather than round (as Delicas are).

❖ Fancy—drops, oval, flowers, leaves, stars, etc. The hole is often at one or both ends rather than through the center.

CHOOSING BEADS

When buying beads, you will see a whole packet or vial of one color. When beading, you are likely to use only one or two beads of the same color next to each other and, as a result, the small dots of each color get lost in the final piece. Though lovely, modern beads are often so subtle in color that they hardly show up at all next to each other; so always choose beads in more contrasting colors than you think you really like. If the beads are in a packet, isolate one corner of each packet and "try" them next to each other to get a better idea of how they will look when stitched together. I'm very fond of the contrast between matte and shiny beads, so I tend to go for this. The colors show up more in beads with a matte finish, and in silver-lined beads, than they do in the transparent or metallic beads. The thread color that may show through transparent beads can alter them quite a bit, so you need to take that into consideration, too.

AMOUNTS NEEDED

It's extremely difficult to judge how many beads you will need to do the projects given in this book because beads vary so much in size and shape. Also, the tension at which you work will probably be different from mine. The number of beads will depend, too, on whether you use a single color or a pattern of two or more colors together.

I've written the instructions in such a way that you can use any type of bead—size 11 seeds or even smaller, tiny cylinders, or 3 cuts—and start off using beads you already have, so you won't have to rush out and buy some. All I can tell you here is that a simple tassel will use from 8 grams of seed or cylinder beads, and could need up to 30 grams—even more —if you want a multiple-beaded skirt and lots of decoration. (Seeds are sold everywhere by the gram.) If you *are* going shopping for beads, buy more than you think you really need for a project, and then make a multi-colored braid, or cover a wooden mold, using the leftovers all mixed up together.

Mixed-color seed and cylinder bead samples, and a small bag showing how transparent beads mix quite well. The yellow inner bag shows through the rainbow-netted outer layer and helps to blend the colors.

MIXING COLORS

Even though the range of colors and finishes you have to choose from is enormous, you will still not always be able to find the exact bead that you want to use. You might wish to graduate gently from one color to another, or make subtle patterns, and "the" bead will elude you. But random mixes can always be used to relieve a plain-colored surface.

Beads are an ideal way of carrying out pointillist effects and optical color mixing, which have been used by painters, printers and embroiderers to deceive the eye into thinking it is seeing a color other than what is really there. I often just add single beads randomly, but the diagrams below will give you a few ideas for patterned and striped effects.

Pauper's mix: If you have small amounts of many different colors left over from previous projects, you can put them all into a small bag—or pot with a lid—and shake them vigorously, and use them to make a braid, fringe, or to cover a mold. I find that you need strongly contrasting beads or the mix will look thin.

The secret of keeping the random look is to spoon out a small amount of beads at a time and use them up—not choosing them but picking them up as they come—and finish that pile before you spoon out any more. The more different colors you have in your mixture, the more effective it can be. You can also mix a number of different shades and tints of one color together.

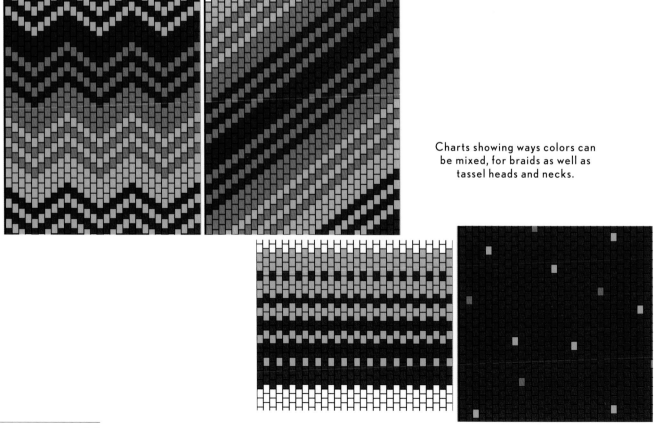

Charts showing ways colors can
be mixed, for braids as well as
tassel heads and necks.

TASSELS

There are normally four parts to a tassel: cord, head, neck and skirt. Sometimes you will want a ruff, used to cover up joins or placed where the cord meets the head. Overskirts can also be made from a fringe of beads, or from smaller tassels hung from the neck. I have used underskirts on some tassels and called these "petticoats": showing through a netted skirt, they give it more body.

Sometimes a tassel has no head, or almost none. It's all neck and skirt. Sometimes there is no skirt, particularly on hard tassels where wooden molds hang on cords and are decorated with beads and paint effects. Humbug tassels are all also neck and no skirt. Any of these parts can be altered, or decorated with all sorts of addition such as frills, hanging loops, or baubles. I have used these names throughout the book as consistently as possible. I've also used the word "collar" to mean a ring of beads, usually a two-bead braid sewn into a ring, used over a cord or around a neck.

TASSEL PROPORTIONS

The proportions, both width and length, of tassel parts can be varied enormously to allow for creativity and character. The neck can be as short as ¼ inch or as long as 3 inches. The skirt can be so short it looks like a frill, or long and elegant.

A tassel can be tiny enough to hang from an ear, or large enough to serve to decorate a drapery tie-back. On the whole, beaded tassels are not huge, as they would be very heavy. Most of those in this book vary from about two or three inches to nine or ten inches long.

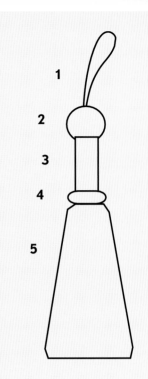

The parts of a tassel:
1. cord
2. head
3. neck
4. ruff
5. skirt

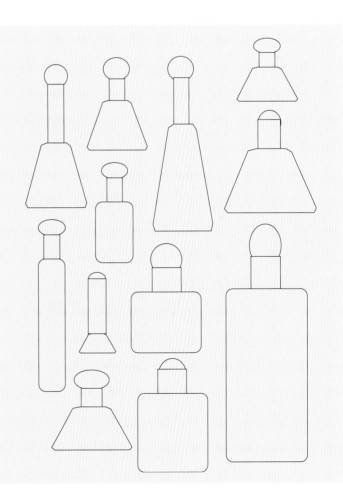

A change in proportion can give character and individuality to a tassel.

TWISTED CORDS

Bead tassels usually need only short, fine cords. These can be easily made by using a pencil and a wooden ball with a hole in it. If, however, you can manage to find a proper cord winder, you will be able to make much longer lengths quite easily, and the results will be truly professional-looking.

If you are making more than a single cord, count the number of twists you do so that each cord you make will look the same.

SIMPLE METHOD

You need a warping post clamped to a table, or the use of a door handle or window latch.

Measure double the length of yarn that you will need for the cord, plus a bit extra. Loop it around the post and tie the two ends together. You can really only do short lengths using this method, but that is all you will need. Take the tied ends through the hole in the wooden ball and insert a pencil into the loop. Holding the ball, twist the pencil with the forefinger of your other hand until there is enough twist. Bring the two ends of the cord together, folding it in half, keeping it under tension with your other hand—you may need some help with this. Allow the cord to twist, stroking it to even out the twist. Knot the two ends together.

CORD WINDER METHOD

Cord winders have three or four hooks, to make two-, three-, or four-ply cords from yarns of any fiber or from already twisted

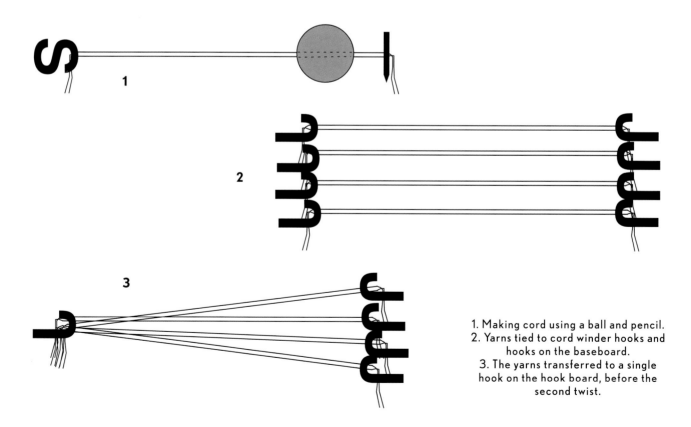

1. Making cord using a ball and pencil.
2. Yarns tied to cord winder hooks and hooks on the baseboard.
3. The yarns transferred to a single hook on the hook board, before the second twist.

yarn. You will probably wish to make the cord from the same yarn as the skirt, if you have one. Four-strand cords look the best.

It's possible to make a cord from four single strands of yarn, but it is easier if they are doubled, or trebled, depending on the thickness of the cord. Clamp the board with the hooks onto the back of a chair or the edge of a door, then lay the cord winder on the seat of a chair or on the floor some distance away. Push the restraining catch into its hole.

Tie one end of the yarn(s) to one of the hooks on the board, walk to the cord winder and loop the yarn around a corresponding hook and then back again to the same hook on the board. Tie the two ends together securely. Do not leave long lengths of yarn hanging, as they will twist with each other and ruin the process.

Do the same for the other sets of hooks, so that you now have four separate lengths of yarn tied to four hooks. Keep the same tension on all the yarns, which should be parallel. Hold the cord winder at waist level, under tension, and turn the handle. Each hook should turn separately to twist the yarn; the head does not revolve. The number of turns will depend on the length of yarn and the amount of twist wanted on the final cord. You will feel the cord winder being pulled away from you, and the yarn should kink

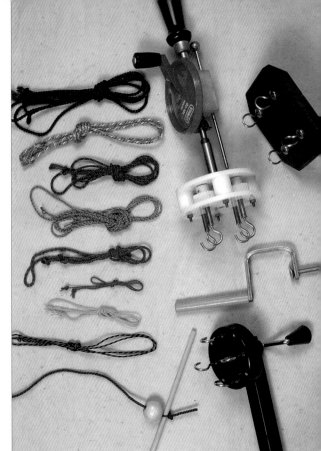

Cords, and the cord winder they were made on.

a bit. More twist means a firmer cord.

With the cord winder hanging over the back of the chair, under tension, transfer all the yarn to a single hook on the hook board.

Go back to the winder and remove the restraining catch. Continue winding slowly in the same direction, still keeping the yarn under tension. The whole head now revolves and the four sets of yarn will twist around each other. Turn until the entire length is twisted, and then a bit more. It does not matter if there is too much twist, because it will drop out when you take it off the hooks. Lift the cord off the hooks and tie a knot at each end to prevent it from unwinding.

Yarn colors: You can use more than one yarn or color on each hook, depending on the thickness of the final cord. If you are using a mixture of yarns, some will stretch while you are winding and will need to be tightened and knotted again.

TASSELMAKING

Basic tassels are simple to make and can be decorated with a beaded neck, ruff, or fringed skirt. I am providing here three methods of tasselmaking that I use in different circumstances.

Many of the tassels in this book are made by simply pulling a cord, a hank of yarn looped through it, gently but firmly through a bead or a tube of beading, so that the fold of yarn comes just to the top of the bead or the tube. The tassel should be quite hard to pull through; if it isn't, add more yarn. The bead or the tube of beading is the only thing that is holding the tassel together and it should be a tight fit.

TASSEL 1

For a different-looking tassel, include a wrapped neck. Wind the yarn around a wire frame, a piece of card, or a wooden skirt board until it is thick enough. Keep a count of the number of windings, if you wish to make more than one of the same size.

Method

Select a length of twisted cord and knot the two raw ends together. Then thread a needle with a sewing thread of the same color, and stitch through both ends, wrapping the thread around the cords between stitches. Once you have it really secured, you can finish the thread and then cut the knot off. The stitching and wrapping will keep it together.

Cut right through the yarns along one edge of the frame, and loop them through the cord with the stitched ends underneath the fold of the bundle of yarns.

Lay the tassel on the table with the cord to the right and the skirt to the left. Cut a length of strong thread in a contrasting color, fold it in half, and lay the loop

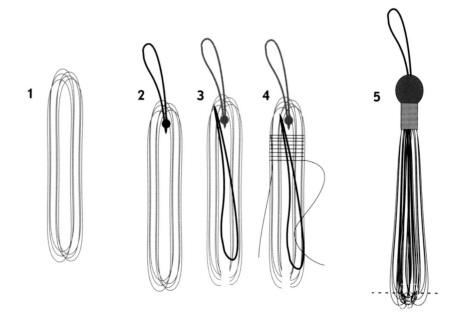

Tassel 1 stages: wrapping the yarn, adding the cord and the loop, adding the spare loop, and wrapping the neck with the end of the wrapping thread pulled up under the wrapping with the loop. The finished tassel has the yarn pulled up into a bead with a large hole. The skirt is trimmed as shown by dashes.

halfway down the length of the skirt, with both ends on the right-hand side at the top of the tassel.

Cut another length of yarn, either the same or a contrasting color, and lay one end at the bottom of the skirt on the left. Pick up the whole tassel, holding the ends of the yarn under your left thumb.

Take the other end of the wrapping yarn and wind it tightly around the neck of the tassel, starting from the top at the right-hand side. Wind for at least ¼ or ½ inch, then tuck the end through the loop on the left. Without letting go of the tassel, pull the two cut ends of the loop. They will disappear under the wrapped neck, pulling the end of the wrapping yarn to the top of the tassel. Cut them off.

TASSEL 2

This tassel is made right on a cord, the ends enclosed within the tassel head.

Method

Lay the hank of yarn on the table. Select a length of twisted cord and knot the two raw ends together. Thread a needle with a sewing thread the same color and stitch through both ends, wrapping the thread around the cords between stitches. When it is really secure, finish the thread and cut the knot off.

Lay the cord along the middle, with the loop to the right of the hank and the stitched ends just to the left of the center point. Wrap the whole bundle as in the tassel 1 method. Pick up the cord and cut through all the loops. Let the yarn fall down and smooth the fold at the top of the tassel head. The yarn should be evenly distributed around the cord. Wrap the neck as before and trim the bottom.

Wrapping yarns on wire frames, card or skirt boards to make tassels.

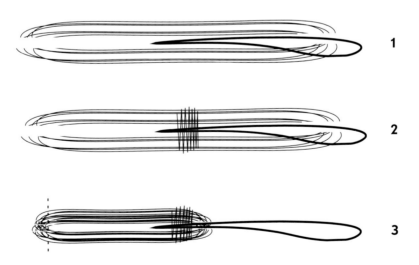

1

2

3

Tassel 2 stages: The loops are cut at both ends and the cord laid inside them, the first wrapping secures the cord, and the second wrapping makes the tassel.

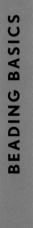
TASSEL 3

These long, narrow tassels are made differently from most, with half the skirt pulled through the central hole of a roll of paper and allowed to fall down again around the outside of the tassel like a waterfall. Wrapping around the outside of the head secures it. These tassels are always long and elegant, without fullness.

Lynn Horniblow worked out how to do this tassel by examining the Chinese tassels in her collection. Some of the heads, even the flat oval ones, were made of wood, but many were made of rolled paper. Some of my Chinese tassels are made another way, similar to tassel method 2.

Method

Wrap a skirt board, or a card or wire frame, counting the number of wraps. You will need to estimate the number of wraps the first time you make the tassel, as the bundle must fit quite tightly inside the paper head. Tie a thread around the loops at each side of the board and slip the hank off carefully. Working on a flat table from now on, hold the two cut ends of the cord together and wrap them tightly. Place the ends of the cord about 1 inch to the left of the center of the hank, with the loop on the right, and distribute the yarn evenly around the cord. Wrap around the whole bundle very tightly, making sure the cord stays in the middle of the bundle.

Attach a sling to the loop of the cord and pull it and the thread, tying the loops together through the central hole of the paper head. Remove the two tying threads, and cut through the loops at both ends.

Hold the tassel up by the cord and allow the yarn loops to fall down around the outside of the tassel. Distribute the yarn evenly around the outside of the head, combing it to make sure it is smooth.

Hold it firmly in your left hand and wrap the whole head with a fine contrasting yarn.

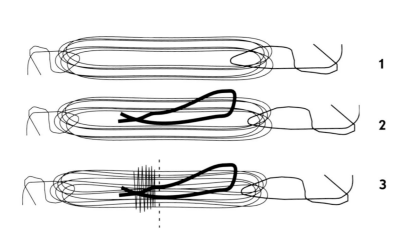

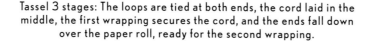

Tassel 3 stages: The loops are tied at both ends, the cord laid in the middle, the first wrapping secures the cord, and the ends fall down over the paper roll, ready for the second wrapping.

WORKING ON BEADS

BLEACHING

If you have some old beads that are dirty, or especially with a silver lining that has become tarnished, you can use bleach to improve their look. The bleaching will totally remove the dirt...and the bead's silver lining, which cannot be replaced. However, you'll have a usable bead or bugle.

Method

In a glass or dish, mix household bleach with an equal amount of water Tip your beads into it and stir them around. Leave them for about half an hour and stir again. If you can still see the silver lining, or if the beads are still dirty, leave them longer. I have bleached some very stubborn beads all day, stirring them occasionally, and they came to no harm. Rinse the beads well under the tap.

ETCHING

There is now an etching fluid available which can turn your shiny beads matte. This is wonderful for extending the range of the beads you already have, and it works on glass beads, opaque or transparent. Warning: It does remove any surface finishes (such as AB, or rainbow, or a metallic finish), but it's a small price to pay for the extra contrast. I always keep a good supply of the original beads to use with the etched beads later on.

Method

Tip your beads into a small plastic pot and cover them with the etching fluid. Stir frequently. After about 15 minutes, pour the beads into a plastic strainer over another plastic pot, and rinse really thoroughly under a tap. The etching fluid can be poured back into the bottle and reused. Turn the beads out onto some kitchen paper and allow them to dry. (The beads can be safely left in the fluid for much longer, should you remember an errand or forget the time.)

You won't see results until the beads dry, so you may be tempted to let them sit in the fluid longer—they'll still look shiny, but that's just because they're still wet.

If you don't rinse the beads enough, you'll notice a white residue on the surface. (Its quite attractive actually, but rubs off.) When you see the residue, just rinse the beads again, more thoroughly.

A sampler of fringe strands, using shiny beads and sequins contrasting with the same beads matted using the etching technique.

PAINTING BEADS AND MOLDS

You can often find wooden beads and molds for tassel heads but, of course, you want them to be a particular color, maybe with a special surface finish. This can be done easily using acrylic, metallic, or enamel paints. There are also many products on the market, such as metallic creams or waxes, intended for touching up mirrors and picture frames, that cannot help but add a special luster when used on top of paint. There are mediums for marbling and distressing, or that will give a crackled or verdigris finish. All can be used to give you just the color you want to go with the glass beads you have chosen.

Method

For a smooth, colored surface, choose an enamel or a paint that does not show brush marks—it will say so on the container. Stick a wooden skewer or chopstick through the bead or wooden mold you want to paint and find something—a glass jar or tin—to prop it up while it is drying.

Paint your bead—giving it two thin coats rather than just one thick one—and allow it to dry thoroughly between the coats. I usually paint a number of beads and tassel heads in various colors so that they are all ready for me to add different finishes later on.

METALLIC CREAMS

These come in different-colored golds, copper, bronzes...even red and blue. They're intended to be used to touch up worn gilded wood, but a little rubbed over the painted beads will add a lovely single- or multi-colored luster. These creams can also be used on untreated wood, but two coats will most likely be needed because the first coat will sink in and go slightly blotchy. Allow to dry, and then rub with a soft cloth to polish. I have even used metallic shoe polish, which is fine but doesn't come in many colors.

DISTRESSED TASSEL MOLDS

The fashion for distressing is still strong and likely to be with us for some time yet. It's easily done on wooden beads and tassel molds. The trick is to build up a number of layers of color to give a sense of depth and an interesting visually textured surface. The advantage of this method is that if you don't like what you have done, you can always cover it with another layer.

Method

For the first layer, use either acrylic paint, metallic paint, knotting (this transparent brown varnish used by woodworkers gives a lovely amber glow), glass paint (a transparent, emulsion paint, especially white), or one of the strong-colored nail polishes, or varnishes, you can buy now. After you have applied the first coat, you may need to rub the wood with steel wool in order to smooth off any rough fibers.

For the second layer, use any of the above paints in a color different from the first layer, but as soon as you have applied it, dab at or rub the paint with a wad of kitchen towel or smooth fabric until enough paint is removed to allow patches of the first color to show through.

For the third layer, use gold cream or wax rubbed in well so that the colors underneath show through; or use clear or colored varnish, or glass or metallic paints. Again, dab or rub the paint so most of it comes off and you can see the underneath layers.

I usually finish off the bead or tassel mold with a layer of acrylic wax. This gives me a finish with a wonderful wax polish-like gleam, which I prefer over the shiny plastic look you get from varnish.

Wooden tassel molds made from a number of different-colored woods and some painted and distressed.

VERDIGRIS

Verdigris is the patina that develops on copper, brass, or bronze—a sort of rust. The verdigris has a very distinctive blue-green coloring which is instantly recognizable. Look at old Chinese bronze vessels or old weapons or bronze statues to see what verdigris should look like.

To reproduce this effect, kits are available that include a metallic—gold, copper, or bronze—base, and a green or blue patina medium to paint on over the base.

Follow the instructions *exactly*, being careful *not* to get the patina too even. You want it to look natural when it develops as it dries.

If you cannot find a kit, you can simulate the effect with acrylic paints, using the method given above for distressed effects, wiping the acrylic paint off to leave a bloom or streaks of blue-green.

MARBLING

Marbling is lovely to look at, but the preparation can be a nuisance. If you choose a spirit-based metallic paint, you can marble on cold water—which is much less trouble. Other metallic paints, however, cannot be used that way; they sink under the water rather than stay on the surface.

Method 1

Fill a shallow tray with water. Shake your jars of liquid metallic paint well to mix them properly. Using a brush, apply the different colors to the surface of the water. Stir with a wooden skewer to swirl the paints into patterns. These are not as controllable as they would be on a special marbling base, but if you use enough colors—at least three different ones—the results are lovely.

Select a painted bead or tassel mold— the dark colors are especially effective under marbled patterns—and fit it onto the end of a drinking straw, or wooden rod, or skewer. Roll it onto the marbled paint, starting to roll before you touch the paint to avoid a hard line. Keep rolling until the bead or head is covered with the color, and prop it up in a pot to dry. If there are missed areas or a hard line where the pattern begins, you can marble it again.

Another way to achieve a marbled effect even more like the "real thing" is to use cling film over thick paint. This method causes slight ridges and shiny areas that contrast nicely with matte ones, so I don't put any varnish on these molds because it would add shine all over.

Method 2

Paint the tassel mold with a plain color and allow to dry. Mix some acrylic paint with a little water if necessary; it should be thick enough to hold its shape and not flow. Dab the paint onto the tassel mold quite thickly but not covering the whole thing—allow the underneath color to show through.

Take a piece of cling film and press it onto the surface of the mold, pressing and pinching it to make ridges and folds in the film. Allow the paint to dry and then peel the cling film off.

Tassel molds marbled with metallic paint (both methods) and some with different verdigris finishes.

GILDED MOLDS

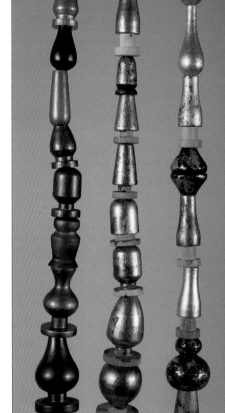

Gold leaf is easy to apply to wooden beads and tassel molds, and gives a wonderful gleam and depth of richness that is not obtainable any other way. The leaf comes in a number of different golden colors; and there's also silver or white gold. Schlag, another name for Dutch metal or metal leaf, is made from brass and will tarnish unless it is varnished. The metal leaf comes in gold, silver, copper, and some lovely variegated colors produced by heating.

I use the transfer leaf on a paper backing, and the real gold and silver are easier to handle than the metal leaf. The mold must be painted first and, if you want a distressed surface, choose a paint color that will enhance the metal coloring. You can use acrylic paint or what is known as a specialist base (usually brick red or yellow).

Method

Cover the wood with two coats of acrylic paint or base color and allow to dry. You might need to rub the mold gently with a fine sandpaper to smooth any roughness in the wood. Next, cover the mold with a coat of gold water-based thin glue called "size" and allow it to dry for 15 minutes or until it becomes tacky. (Size does not dry com-

pletely for about thirty hours, so you could actually leave it some hours before continuing, even overnight—that's the way size is. Working with it is wonderful!)

Gently press the gold or metal leaf onto the mold with a paintbrush or your fingers. If there are any gaps, pick up some leaf flakes and press them on, where needed. Don't try to remove overlapping bits of leaf until the whole thing has dried completely.

After leaving the mold to dry overnight, rub the gilded mold with a soft cloth to remove tiny bits and smooth the mold off. If you are using metal leaf, it will need to be varnished *immediately* with a clear varnish or shellac to keep it from tarnishing.

More color can be added, if you wish, using metallic creams or an amber varnish, such as the knotting or button polishes used by woodworkers. The gold leaf gleams through these in a way that paint can never do.

Molds covered with gold and metal leaf, some using flakes of different-colored leaf and others rubbed with metallic creams.

THE STITCHES

Beading has a long history. Stitches that we tend to think of as, for example, worked in Africa for the last hundred years were used in Britain during the seventeenth century. Netting is a quite universal stitch, used extensively in China, India, Malaysia, and South Africa. "Peyote" stitch was obviously not called that in 2200 B.C.! Such names are convenient, but can be misleading. People therefore often prefer using a word that describes the structure of the stitch (such as "lattice" or "brick") rather than another name. In this book, I tend to do the same.

I'm a firm believer in simplification. If a process is simple, it gives your creativity free reign. If a process is complex, you spend so much time and effort working it out that little time is left for other things or for just enjoying what you're doing. Therefore, I also tend to use very few stitches in my work, mainly peyote and netting, but sometimes brick or square stitch. The handling and flexibility of the stitches are different, and each should be used accordingly. Double and treble versions of stitches behave much the same way as single versions. Beading using matte beads is less flexible than when using shiny beads.

Finally, the tension at which you will personally come to work naturally will be slightly different from the working tension others will use, so this must also be taken into account in your beading.

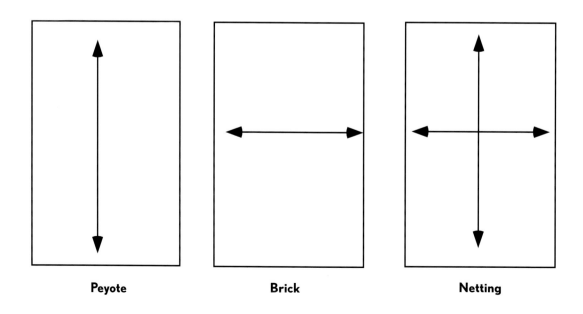

Peyote **Brick** **Netting**

Diagram showing the direction of flexibility
in different stitches.

STITCH CHARACTERISTICS

Peyote stitch, if worked flat, is stiff horizontally, as you work it, but very flexible going from top to bottom. Brick stitch is the opposite, so if you made a small bag in brick stitch you could not have a continuous piece for a flap because it would not fold over properly. Tubular brick stitch is perfect for tassel necks, but so is peyote stitch if worked flat and stitched together into a tube—when it will hold the shape of the neck as well as tubular brick stitch. Horizontal netting is stiffer from side to side than is vertical netting, so while it is a good stitch for a tassel skirt that flares, vertical netting is better if you want to cover a wooden tassel mold or control a flyaway skirt. You can tie a peyote stitch strip into a knot, but square stitch is even better because it is flexible in both directions, so it is also better for stuffed shapes—like the humbugs in this book.

Some stitches, like netting, expand widthwise, and you can make use of this to control the shape without increasing or decreasing it. However, if you increase the number of beads in netting, it simply drops downward—good for a skirt, but not if you are trying to make a ball shape.

So, on the whole, you use the stitch you like doing and adapt it, or the instructions, accordingly. I've chosen particular stitches for each project, but that does not mean you *must* use the same one. Use whichever stitch you like and work with it, bearing in mind the characteristics of that stitch. If a stitch is too floppy for a tassel neck, then stiffen it with a card cylinder (painted the same color so it does not show). Work the stitch flat and wrap it tightly around the cylinder before joining the edges. Or, pull an even larger hank of thread through it to stiffen it.

An exception is when covering wooden tassel molds. You need a flexible stitch for this, so I have used netting. But you could try a flower-chain fabric, which is equally flexible.

A bag showing how flexible netting is in size 14 beads contrasting with bands of stiffer beading, and 4-bead peyote strips knotted, showing the vertical flexibility of the stitch.

BRICK STITCH

As its name suggests, this is beading in a brick pattern, looking like peyote stitch sideways on. It is good for bags, boxes and bowls, jewelry and tassel necks. It can be worked in single, double, or treble form—the latter two are actually quicker to do than the single. The brick stitch seems to be the one that most people find easiest, especially in tubular form. Its great advantage is that, when worked flat, it naturally decreases into a triangle shape that is most useful for flaps and three-dimensional shapes.

TUBULAR METHOD

Start with a 2-bead strip of peyote stitch, as shown below. Join the strip into a ring by folding the strip in half, taking the needle down through the first two beads and back up the last two beads. Pull tight.

To brick stitch, pick up a bead, take the needle under the loop between the first two beads of the row beneath, and take the needle back through the bead you have picked up, going back into the hole you just came out of. You can work upwards or downward, but each bead you pick up should sit with the hole in the same direction as the first two rows. If it does not, then you have gone back through the bead from the wrong side.

Pick up a bead, and take the needle under the loop and then back through the bead. Continue up to the end of the row. Join the last bead to the first one by attaching both beads together. You are ready to start the next row.

Complete each row before you begin another, or you are likely to find a hole appearing in the stitching.

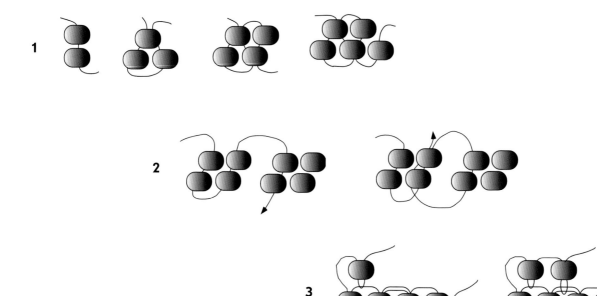

How to do brick stitch tubing.

FLAT METHOD

If you wish to make a flat piece of beading, start every row by picking up two beads, taking the needle under the first loop and then back through the second bead. See diagram below. This method will give stepped outside edges to the beading.

Tassel using brick stitch cylinders and tiny peyote beads. The colors are mixed gradually so that they blend into each other.

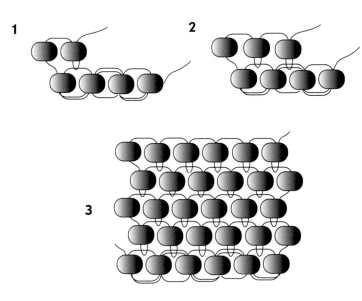

How to do flat method brick stitch.

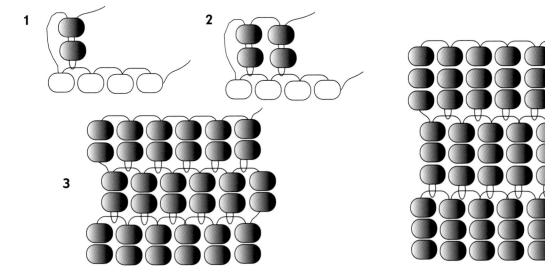

How to do double and treble brick stitch.

PEYOTE STITCH

Even-count peyote, whether worked flat or in a tube, is used for many of the projects in this book, so that is the only method I give here. If you are new to the stitch, try working it in two colors, as in the diagram, so that you can see which bead to go through next.

Tubular peyote is much easier to do on a support. This can be a dowel rod, a pencil, a wooden knitting needle, or a skewer—even a short piece of broomstick. I have collected, over the years, a number of different-sized rods. Even so, sometimes I cannot find the exact size I need. You can even use a drinking straw, if it is supported by another one—simply make a slit along the length of a straw and squeeze and insert it into an intact one to serve as the stiffener.

A good, if expensive, idea is to buy a complete set of bamboo knitting needles. That is one way to be sure of getting every size of narrow rod you could possibly wish for. Look around the various sections of large craft or hardware stores. You will find rods in the most unlikely places. Wood is the best material to use; plastic and metal are too smooth.

FLAT PEYOTE (EVEN COUNT)
Start with a 4-bead strip to learn the stitch, but the method is the same for any number of beads.

Method
Pick up a light-colored bead and take the needle through it again to anchor it. Then pick up a dark bead, another light one, and another dark one. There are four beads on your thread.

Pick up another dark bead and go back through the third bead, pulling the thread tight so that the two dark beads form a T-shape. Pick up another dark bead and go through the first bead.

Continue adding two dark and two light beads alternately, making a flat strip with two light and two dark lines. You should hold your thread tightly between each stitch; otherwise, the whole band will become loose and floppy. I grab the thread between two fingers of my left

Tassel in peyote stitch with picots on the strips (Ann Mockford).

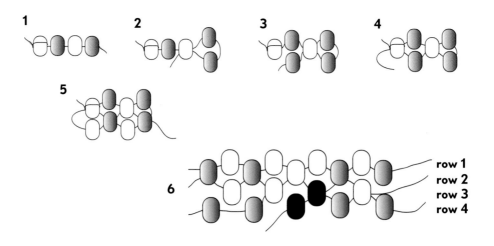

row 1
row 2
row 3
row 4

How to do peyote stitch.

hand and only let go at the last minute of pulling the thread through a bead.

TUBULAR PEYOTE (EVEN COUNT)

Although this is slightly trickier to do than odd-count peyote in a tube, you will be rewarded by smooth top and bottom edges, essential for tassels, so it is worth persevering.

Method

String on an even number of beads to go around a supporting rod, starting with one bead that is a different color from any of the others. This color will spiral around the tube, reminding you when you come to the end of each round, which is where you are most likely to make a mistake. Take the needle through the beads again, making them into a ring. Slip the ring onto the support with the working thread coming from the right-hand side. Pull the thread tight and knot the ends together, leaving a tail at least 8 inches long. Wind this tail around the rod above the beading

and secure it by winding an elastic band over it.

Take the needle through the first bead (the one that is a different color), then pick up a bead of the same color to start the new row. Take the needle through the next bead down. Continue working the peyote stitch in the main color until you come to the end of the round. Go through the last TWO beads of the different color, pick up a bead the same color, and continue doing the round in the main color.

TWO- AND THREE-DROP PEYOTE

Even quicker than single peyote are two- and three-drop peyote, which are both done the same way except that two, three, or even more beads are picked up and treated as a single bead while working the stitch. They can be worked both flat or tubular.

To increase, you change from two-drop to three-drop peyote and back again to two-drop and then single peyote.

A tassel showing single- and four-drop peyote, with ruffs of multiple loops. The necks of the small tassels are wrapped in the center of a hank of yarn folded in half and wrapped again to make the neck.

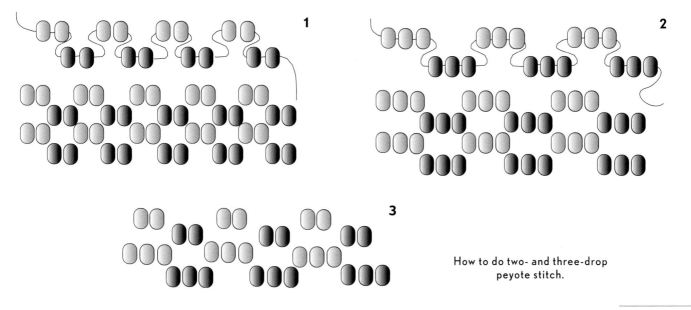

How to do two- and three-drop peyote stitch.

Method

Pick up an even number of beads, a number that is divisible by four, for the first row.

Pick up two more beads, then skip two beads and pick up the next two. Continue working, picking up two and going through two beads every time.

PEYOTE FRILLS AND RUFFLES

The peyote stitch is the best stitch to make frills and ruffles, either on necks, or over beaded balls or molds, or to make the tiny flowers or cups given in the trimmings section, on page 109.

There are two methods shown here, the first gradually increasing to make a frill and the second having a steeper increase to make a ruffle.

Method 1

Add two beads between each bead on the previous row, and then work two rows adding only one bead between each bead. If you wish to make the frill deeper, add two beads between each alternate bead and then work two more rows with one bead between each bead as before.

Method 2

Add two beads between each bead. Repeat for the next row or round, adding two beads between each bead.

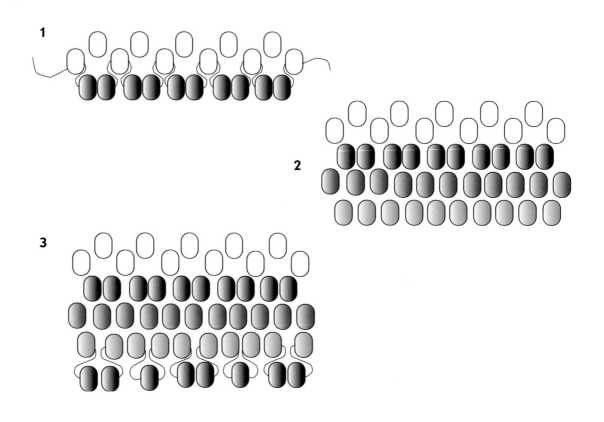

How to make frills and ruffles using methods 1 and 2.

NETTING

Most of the netting done in this book will be worked horizontally, to hold its shape well for tassel skirts.

A net, with its distinct diamond pattern, is usually stitched using an odd number of beads with a central, or "spot," bead of a different color. However, netting worked using an even number of beads is fine, counting the two central beads as if they were one.

This gives more flexibility when you are trying to make a skirt an exact shape—not too full and not too narrow. Net can be worked using a bugle instead of a few beads, or with a larger spot bead, or a bead of a different shape, such as a cube or triangle.

Netting can also be worked on a single line of beads, or on the bottom row of peyote stitch using the down beads, or on brick stitch. I usually work netting horizontally around a rod.

Tassel with frills coiling around bead-covered balls and tiny flowers at the bottom of the fringe (Ann Mockford).

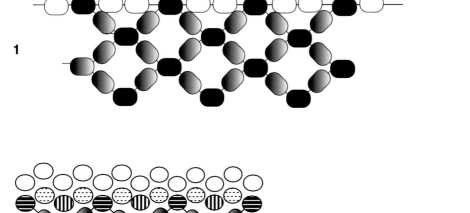

How to do netting on:
1. a string of beads
2. the edge of peyote stitch
3. the edge of brick stitch

Method

For a 5-bead net, with the needle coming out of a bead, pick up 2 beads, a spot bead and 2 more beads. Then, leaving a gap, take the needle through the next available bead. Pick up 5 beads again and, leaving a similar gap, go through the next bead.

When you reach the end of every round, make sure you take the bead forward through 3 beads to start the next round.

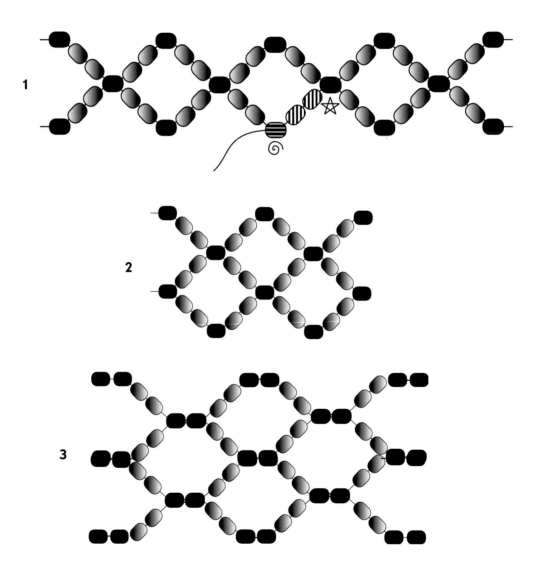

How to:
1. finish a row and move on to the next
2. do 5-bead netting
3. do 6-bead netting

VERTICAL NETTING

Vertical netting is a very supple fabric, more flexible than if netting is done horizontally. It can be used for controlling flyaway skirts and for covering tassel molds or balls. It can be worked as a piece in the hand, or hung from peyote stitch.

Method

String the number of beads that you will need for the length of the first row. If you are making a 7-bead net, you will need an odd number of multiples of 7, plus 4 beads, e.g.: 5 times 7 for 35 beads, then plus 4. Making the spot beads a different color simplifies the process.

Follow the diagram, working back and forth until you have a piece of netting the size you want.

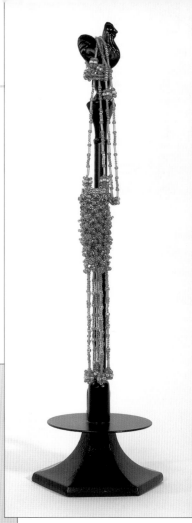

Tiny bag with an outer layer of netting over a brick stitch base and buried bugle fringe.

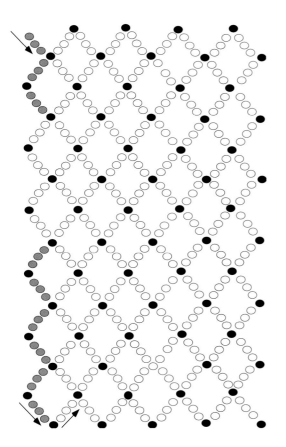

Vertical netting using 5 times 7 beads. Start at the top arrow and work downward, then work back up, joining the second row to the first one at intervals.

Netted bag made using the righthand pattern on page 70. (Ann Mockford)

JOINING BEADING

Many times you will need to join beading into a tube to make tiny beads or necks for tassels. The first two methods are slightly different for brick or peyote stitch, but are invisible when they are done. These methods can also be used to stitch shapes together at the sides in order to cover wood or card pieces. The third method is for joining two edges across a space.

Methods

Join two brick stitch edges by working around and around the beads on each edge, moving down a bead each round."

For joining two peyote stitch edges, work the same number of beads on each row and the edges will "zip" together. Then ladder-stitch them securely.

For joining the sides of peyote stitch across a space, string on three beads, go up through a bead on the other side, down through the next bead, pick up three more beads, and continue.

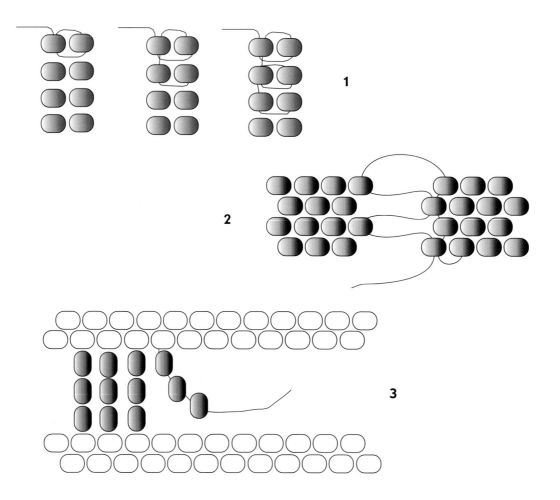

Joining beading on: 1. brick stitch 2. peyote stitch, and
3. adding a bead strip between two pieces of beading to cover shapes.

When you thread your needle in readiness for beading, it's often a good idea not to cut the thread tail from the spool. The spool will stop the beads from sliding off the thread, if and when they are so inclined—which is often. Also, many times you can go back to the beginning of the beading, pull a new length of thread from the spool, put the needle onto it and work backwards from the first beads. This saves you—twice—from having to finish off the thread. As this is not always workable, if you do cut the thread be sure to leave a good long length—about two yards/meters if you can handle it.

When starting off, it's a good idea, if you can, to go through the first bead twice, so that the bead acts as a stopper.

To finish off a thread, if you are in the middle of a piece of beading leave the end of the thread (about 6 inches) hanging. This way you will know where the last bead is that you have gone through. Weave a new thread in, taking it back through the beading in different directions to secure it. A bead woven through beading in one, or even two, directions will pull out. If it is woven back and forth three times, it will stay and there's no need for a knot.

Come out from the same bead as the end of the previous thread and continue beading. Then go back to the other end and weave that through in the same way.

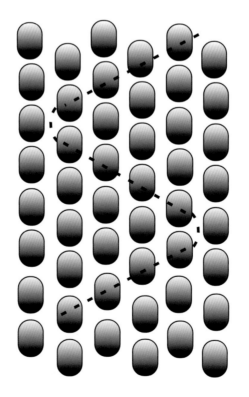

Starting and finishing a thread.

BRAIDS & CORDS

A twisted cord, whether store-bought or homemade, can be enriched by the addition of beads. Here are some possibilities:

✧ Thread a needle and sew the end firmly into the end of the cord. Pick up about 6 beads on your needle and wind the beads around the cord, letting them fit into the groove. Sew through the cord and back through the last bead. Pick up more beads and continue this process.

✧ Make a 2-bead strip and coil it around the cord, attaching it at either end. If the cord is a long one, you will also need to sew the bead strip to the cord at intervals for it to be secure.

✧ Wrap a grouping of beads over the cord at intervals.

If you want to do something about those raw cord endings:

✧ Wrap the end of a cord with yarn to secure the ends; then wind a string of beads over the wrapping and sew both ends of the thread into the cord.

✧ Knot the end of a cord and stitch groups of thread vertically over the knot to hide it. If you are still doubtful about the cut ends of yarn, dab a little PVA glue on them. It will dry clear, so won't really show.

Adding beads to a cord at the top of
the head to finish it.

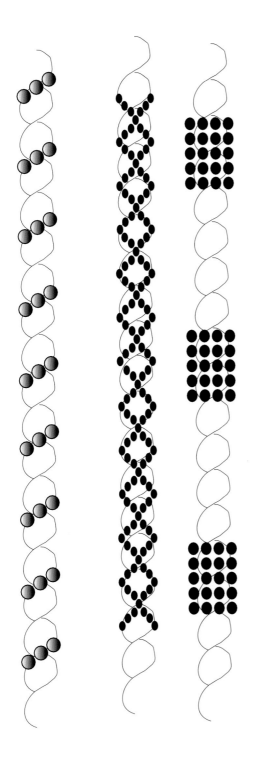

Covering cords with beading.

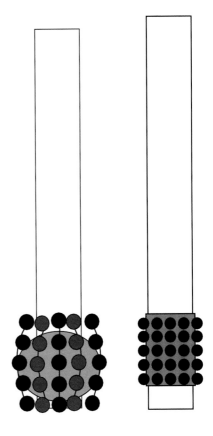

Finishing off cord endings.

BEAD CORDS

Peyote stitch can be used to make cords, and this is probably the only time when I find it really worthwhile to use odd-count peyote, which continues around the cord in a spiral. Tubular odd-count peyote can be used to make a cord without anything inside it or to cover a ready-made cord. The slight bump at the top and bottom, due to using odd-count peyote, hardly shows on a cord.

Any beads can be used to make these cords: seeds, cylinders, or cuts; and they can be any size, although smaller beads do look better. Although these cords are a bit too small to work a pattern, diagonal stripes or shading along the length from one color to another are both extremely effective. See the color mixing charts on page 16.

Short lengths of both these cords can be tied into knots to decorate the necks or skirts of tassels—or to hang tassels from. My granddaughter recently made a brick stitch cord because that is the only stitch she knows, but it is slower to do. The stitch can be used by itself or over a cord and, because it is stiffer than peyote, it is useful as the handle of a bag or tote. A square stitch cord would be more flexible.

Method

Peyote-covered cord: String enough beads to go around a length of piping cord, and take the needle through the beads again to make a ring. There should be an odd number of beads. Work tubular peyote stitch until the cord is covered.

Peyote cord: Pick up 5, 7, or 9 beads and take the needle through all the beads again to make a ring. Work tubular peyote until it is long enough.

Brick stitch cord: Make a 2-bead peyote strip until it is long enough to meet in a circle, with probably about 5 beads each side. Join it into a ring. Work brick stitch into the loops until the cord is long enough.

A variety of bead-covered cords.

ADDING TEXTURE

Netting: A beaded cord can have a netting overlay. Pick up enough beads to go around your cord over the top of the beading, making sure you have a number that is divisible by 3 or 4. Work a 7- or 9-bead netting into every third or fourth bead. It is probably not worth working a smaller netting, because you will hide the original beading.

Picots or loops: After you have made the cord, you can sew extra beads or loops on and they will add "crunch" texture or movement to the cord and strengthen the netting.

Tassels from Afghanistan with beaded cords. Some cords have strung beads coiled around them, and some beads are stitched directly onto the yarn cords.

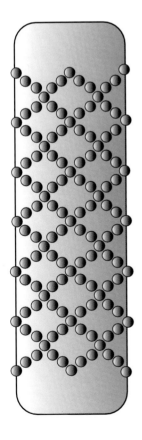 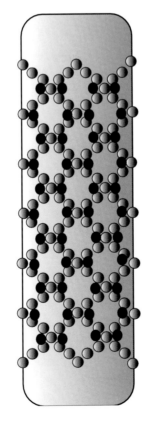 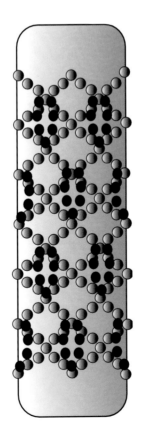

Netting over cords or over bead-covered cords.

BURIED-BUGLE CORDS

Or perhaps it should be "berried-bugle" cords? Anyway, these are quick to do and really show off all those lovely cubes, large cylinders and other fringe beads to perfection. Wrapping beads around other large bugles or beads is not a new technique, but it is given a new slant here, making cords that can be worn as jewelry, used as handles for tiny bags, or serve as fringes for anything.

BEAD MATERIALS

Lots of bugles, beads, cylinders, triangles or any fancy beads, plus seed beads. The nicer the beads, the nicer the cord. Make sure that the bugles do not have sharp edges or they will cut the sewing thread.

If you're using size 11 cylinder beads, you'll find that they often disappear into the hole of a larger bead, so add a size 11 seed bead between the two to act as a stopper.

Method

Put a needle on the end of a very long thread, go through the hole in a bugle or a large bead and tie the two ends together at one end, leaving a 6-inch tail to finish off later.

Then pick up a grouping of 3 to 5 beads that match the length of the large bead or bugle, and take the needle through the hole again. Pick up the same combination of beads again and go through the hole.

I find that about a 5 or 6 grouping of beads is all that you can get through the hole before it is blocked up with thread. Finally, string on some beads for spacers, then another large bead or bugle, and cover it again in the same way.

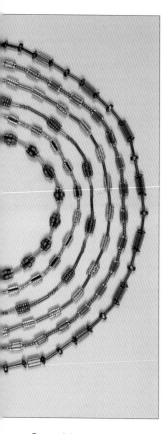

Buried-bugle cords.

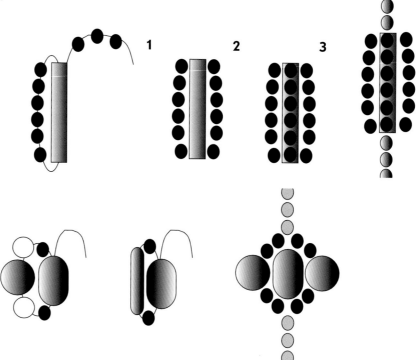

The stages of covering a bugle with beads.

CRAZY CHAIN

This chain was first made by Ann Mockford and is based on one she saw in Malacca, Malaysia, but the original had loops instead of the beaded picots. The picots are worked as you go along, forcing the string into a zigzag. It looks better with the ends looped together, but if you wish to use it and want it to hang straight, don't put a heavy bead on the bottom of the string. It will weight down the chain too much. This chain should be bouncy.

You can use a bugle instead of beads between the picots, and the picot beads could be larger or a different shape, or you could work a 3-bead picot.

Method

Pick up 4 beads. Skip the fourth bead and take the thread back through the third bead again, making a picot. Pick up 6 more beads, skip the sixth bead and take the thread back through the fifth bead again, making a picot. Repeat this row for the length of the loop you wish.

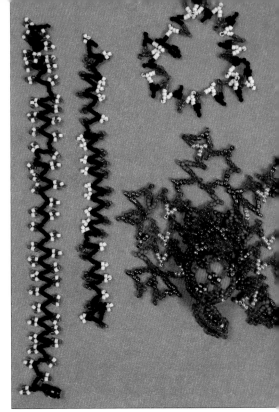

Crazy chains and a tassel using crazy chains as a skirt (Ann Mockford).

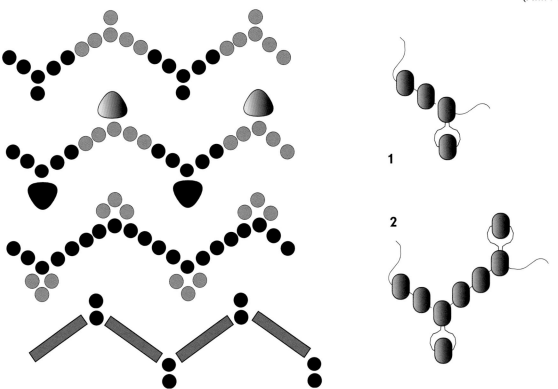

A crazy chain (top), how to make it, and variations using different beads.

FLOWER CHAINS

Delicate strings with loops of beads looking like tiny flowers are not new to us, but they are so adaptable that they deserve to be included in this book. The "flowers" add interest to the hanging strings of beads, and they can be joined together to make a fabric that can be used for a tiny bag or as a tassel skirt. Bugles and different sizes and shapes of beads can be included in these strings, and the distance between the flowers can vary.

Method

String 3 beads, or bugles and beads, then 4 round beads to make the flower. These flower beads look better if they are of a larger size or different color. Take the needle forward through the first flower bead again, making the flower beads into a tight ring. Repeat for the length of the string.

MAKING FABRIC

Follow diagrams 2 and 3 to double up the strings, picking up 3 beads and taking the needle through the third flower bead of the previous string. For the third row, pick up 3 beads, then pick up the flower beads 1 and 2, go through the third flower bead of the previous row, then pick up flower bead 4. Take the needle forward through flower bead 1.

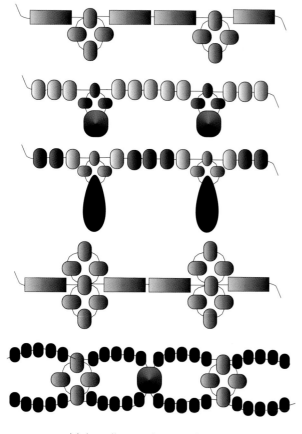

Making flower-chains and braids:
basic method at top.

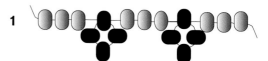

1

2

3

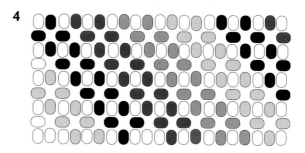

4

Making flower-chain fabrics by joining
braids together.

These tassels are made by attaching a flower-chain skirt onto the neck of a wooden mold that is painted all over because the base of the mold might show through the skirt.

The verdigris tassel has a single layer of fringe, but the bronze tassel has two, because the neck of the mold was so thin that not enough chains could be attached in a single layer. The buried bugles were added only to the layer underneath; more would have given a too-heavy look.

Materials

painted wooden mold, or combination
  of molds
cord
size 11 beads
fringe beads

Method

Fold the cord in half and knot the ends together. Pull the loop through to the top of the mold, using a sling if necessary. Wipe PVA glue on the knot and pull the loop until the knot is hidden just inside the mold. Let dry. Knot the top of the cord.

Skirt: Pick up enough of the beads to go around the neck of the tassel mold, leaving a space the size of one bead so that you can get your needle between them. Take the thread through all the beads again, making a ring. Slip it over the neck of the tassel and pull the thread tight. Tie the ends together in a knot.

Fringe: Plan a single flower-chain for the fringe, which should be at least three times as deep as the mold. Add heavier beads, or buried bugles, at the bottom of the string to add weight.

String one of these chains into every bead around the neck. If the neck is very small and the fringe is a bit thin, add a second layer of fringing. This layer can be shorter if you wish, and have a different set of beads at the bottom of each flower chain. Add a ruff if you wish, following the instructions on page 103, or put a collar around the mold.

Two tassels with flower-chain fringes hung on painted wooden molds (7 inches and 7½ inches)

A tassel (Ann Mockford) showing a flower-chain fabric and two bags using flower chains as fringe. The gray-and-gold bag is made using flower-chain fabric.

FLAT BRAIDS

These simple braids can be used for so many things—to suspend fringe, cover a tassel neck, decorate tassel skirts, make into such trimmings as loops, coils, or knots, make rings for linked chains, or use as a base for ruffs for the final trimming of tassels. Beads are so beautiful now that often all you want for many purposes is simply a plain flat strip of braid; or you can use the color mixing patterns given on page 16.

For most purposes, even-count peyote is simplest, but square stitch, four-sided stitch, or the peyote variation given earlier are more flexible for hanging as tassel overskirts or tying into knots.

The braids can be made using any type of size of bead, even bugles if you wish a more ladder-like look. They can be decorated along the edge with picots or loops or frills, or on the top with beads sewn on—which provides a rich texture.

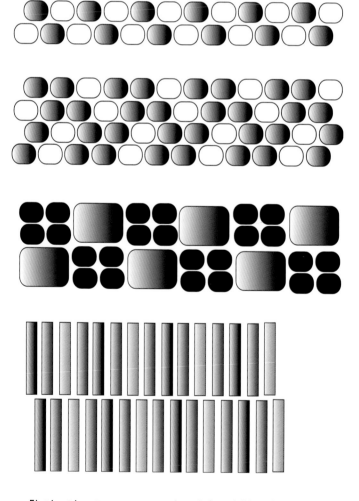

Flat braids using peyote stitch showing different color combinations.

Flat braids using peyote stitch with 2 and 4 beads, and variations using 3.3 cylinders and bugles.

Method

Work 2-, 4-, or 6-bead peyote according to the instructions on pages 30 and 32.

Odd-count peyote will also work if you like doing it, but I find it tiresome to fuss with and keep forgetting the sequence. If I want a narrower braid, I just use smaller beads.

Tassel with flat braids doubled over and stitched to bands of beading.

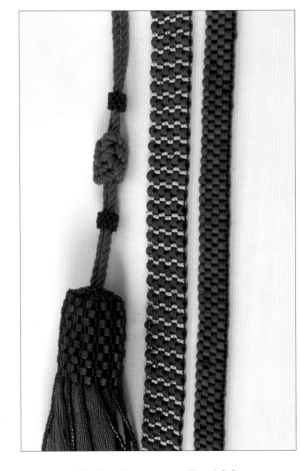

Flat braids using size 11 and 3.3 cylinder beads. The tassel uses the braid to wrap the head (Jackie Dunn).

LARGE BEAD BRAIDS

There are two ways of making these braids, depending on the beads you use. I prefer to do the all-in-one method if possible, but often the holes in the big beads are just too large, or the smaller beads just slip through or partially into them to lie at an odd angle.

The second method will work with anything, but it often needs fiddling with. The main thing is that you get the important accent down the center of the braid, where it has the most impact.

Method 1

Make a 2- or 4-bead peyote strip, counting the number of beads along each side. Make another one to match. Sew them together according to the top diagram below, adding any large bead or combination of beads between the two strips.

Method 2

Make the all-in-one braid shown below, working from side to side and including the large accent beads as you go. You may have to choose your beads carefully for them to stay where you put them!

Detail of large bead braids using 3.3 cylinders, cubes, and drops.

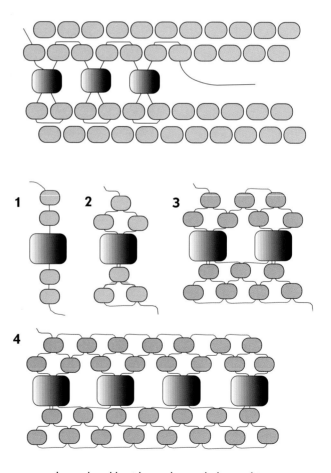

Large bead braids can be made by working narrow strips and joining them together with a large bead, or working the braid all in one piece.

BRAID EDGES

Plain strips of beading, whatever the stitch, can be enhanced by a decorative edging. Simple picots, small single or multiple loops, or larger beads sewn to the edge at intervals all break up the straight edge and can give a contrast of color and shape. You could use triangular, cube, or turban-shaped beads for this.

An even softer look can be given by working small frills along one or both edges. Braid can be used for a loop-strip tasse —or to decorate a small bag.

Method
Single or 3-bead picots are sewn to the edge after the strip is finished. See diagram 1 for sewing beads onto the loops between the beads on the edge of peyote stitch. I prefer sewing extra beads into beads along the edge, see diagrams 2 and 3. It seems to be a stronger method.

Diagram 4 shows how to sew a 5-bead loop onto an edge, and diagram 5 shows a short fringe.

Frills: A frill is more complex and you will need to sew a row of beads along the edge, facing in a different direction, which will act as a foundation row for the frill. Add alternate beads going in one direction along the edge of the peyote strip, and then fill in between them on the return journey.

Braid edges, frills, picots, tiny loops and triangles.

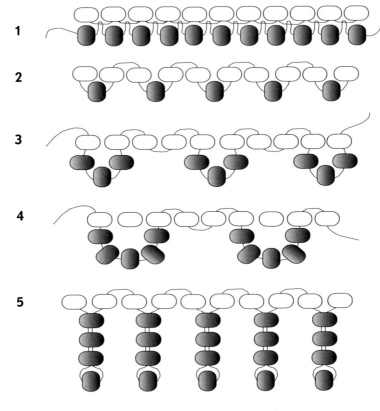

Adding decorative edges
to flat braids.

LYNN'S BRAID

As I really dislike doing odd-count peyote on short rows, whenever I want a 3-bead strip, I make it according to diagram 1 below, picking up one bead on one side of the strip and two beads on the other.

When she was first experimenting with beading techniques, Lynn Horniblow kept trying to figure things out without looking at book instructions. Her attempt at 3-bead peyote turned out the braid shown in diagram 2. It is very flexible and you must keep the tension very tight as you are working it or the whole strip disintegrates! If, however, you can manage it, the result has a wonderful movement when hanging down tassel skirts—just as much, in fact, as strung beads but with more impact because it is wider.

Method

Pick up 5 beads on your needle and go back through bead 2. Pick up 2 more beads, skip 3, and go back through bead 4. Continue this row until the strip is long enough.

Keep the thread taut between two fingers of your left hand all the time you are working, and use a matching color thread as it is inclined to show between the beads.

Two tassels using Lynn's braid hanging down skirts. (Lynn Horniblow's is on the right.)

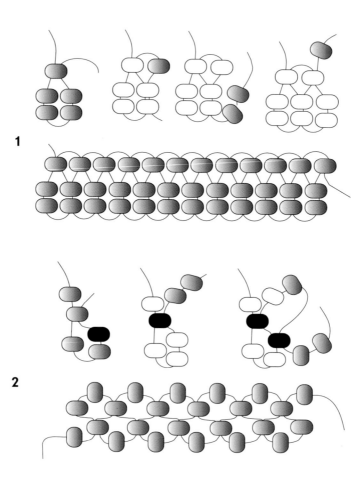

How to make Lynn's braid.

BEAD CHAINS

Strips of beading can be joined into rings and the rings linked together to make chains of enormous variety. The rings can be wide or narrow, short or long, folded in half and doubled, or even have strips of beading threaded through them. They can be used as cords on tassels, worn as necklaces, or added as braid to the edge of a bag or cushion. The small size of the rings rules out any complex pattern, but stripes of different-colored beads are easily incorporated or random color mixes can be used.

Materials

seed or cylinder beads, size 11 or smaller

Method

Basically, what you do is make a 4-bead strip of peyote stitch about 1½ inch long. Join the two ends together and finish the thread off. Then, make a second strip the same size but before joining the ends, pass one end of the strip through the link you have already made. Then join the ends.

Some people go merrily on, making endless links, and forget about linking them! If this should happen to you, it's a case of making more strips and passing the strip through two links before joining the ends.

A variety of bead chains.

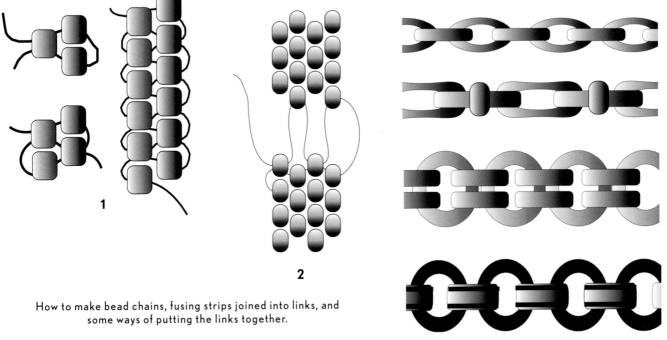

How to make bead chains, fusing strips joined into links, and some ways of putting the links together.

VARIATIONS

Endless variations of these chains are possible, using different widths and lengths of each chain.

❖ Make 2 narrow links and treat them as one.

❖ Make alternate short and long links.

❖ Make a tiny strip and wrap it around a link to alter the shape, and then join the ends.

❖ Make many links and then thread them together with a very long, plain strip of beading, about a yard long. The strip goes back and forth through the links, keeping them in a brick pattern, and passing through each link twice. See right-hand chain in photo on page 53.

❖ Make extra-long links, fold them in half, and pass the joining link through both end loops.

Dumbbells with bead-rolled molds joined
with chain links
(Lynn Horniblow).

RING CHAIN TASSEL

Peyote stitch is used for these rings because it is flexible along the length of the beading, which goes horizontally around the neck of the tassel. It is also flexible when going vertically down the length of the neck so that the beading bends in and out of the spaces when secured by the tiny rings. This direction of flexibility is also necessary for the looped and folded rings that hold the three over-tassels.

Materials
seed or cylinder beads in 2 or 3 colors
yarn for the cord

Method
First, make all the rings as follows:
3 horizontal rings = 6 beads wide, 28 beads long, counted on one edge
3 long vertical rings = 4 beads wide, 60 beads long, counted on one edge
9 tiny securing rings = 2 beads wide, 12 beads long, counted on one edge
3 twisted rings for over-tassels = 2 beads wide, 40 beads long, counted on one edge.

Join the 3 horizontal rings, fitting the beads together like the teeth of a zipper. Loop a long vertical ring over the three horizontal ones, and join the ends. Loop a tiny securing ring around the long one between two of the vertical rings, and join the ends. Repeat with the other two tiny securing rings.

To prevent the bottom ring from falling off, join a twisted ring, fold it in half, and loop it through the bottom of one long ring. Tie temporarily with string. Repeat with the other two.

Make a cord about 10 to 12 inches long. Wrap both sets of cut ends together extremely tightly, making a loop.

Wrap enough threads for the tassel, about 18 inches long. Fold them in half through the loop of the tassel, covering the ends. Comb to even them.

Push the cord up through the beading, and pull the tassel up until it just shows at the top.

Spread the beading out evenly around the tassel neck.

Make 3 smaller over-tassels and pull them through the twisted rings, removing the string to do so. Make rings 6 beads wide and long enough to fit tightly around the neck. Then just comb and trim the skirt.

The ring chain tassel (9 inches) and another using links to pull up the netted skirt, making it look like a double layer.

Putting rings together for ring chain tassel.

BOOKMARKS

You can use any flat braid for a bookmark, but these are worked in peyote stitch, which is flexible along its length so that it falls out of the book with grace. The length varies according to book size; ideally a couple of inches longer than a page.

These bookmarks use small amounts of a number of different colors, shading into each other to give gentle gradations even of strongly contrasting colors—so you can use up beads left over from other projects. The dark strip down the side holds all the colors together, and the ends can be straight or shaped, and with or without a fringe. (If you won't be adding a fringe, make the bookmark four or five inches longer.)

The beads should be very even in size or the edges will not be straight and smooth. If there is a problem with the edging, finish it off with a row of spaced beads to hide the unevenness.

Here is a simple project to start now.

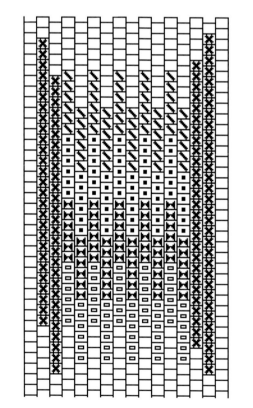
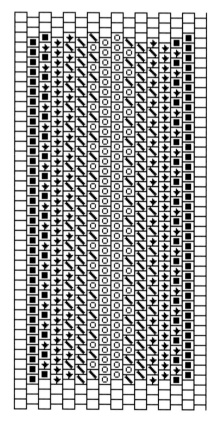

Charts for three possible flat-braid patterns using several bead colors.

Materials

seed or cylinder beads in three colors

Method

Using a very long thread, pick up 14 beads in the dark edging color. Here we use A for the dark color and B and C for the other two colors in the project. Work peyote stitch on alternate beads following the instructions below for shading the colors into each other or the chart shown below.

After the edging, work 10 rows using 1A, 5B, 1A, then

11. 1 row 1A, 5C, 1A
12. 1 row 1A, 5B, 1A
13. 1 row 1A, 5C, 1A
14. 2 rows 1A, 5B, 1A
15. 2 rows 1A, 5C, 1A
16. 1 row 1A, 5B, 1A
17. 2 rows 1A, 5C, 1A
18. 1 row 1A, 5B, 1A

Work 10 rows 1A, 5C, 1A. Then repeat pattern rows 11 to 18, either in that order *or in reverse.* You can change one of the inner colors if you wish.

Finish with 2 rows of the dark, A edging, or add a fringe.

Bookmarks using wide flat braids.

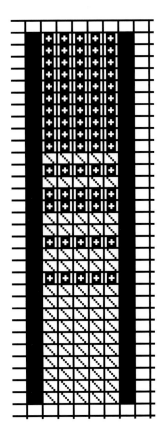

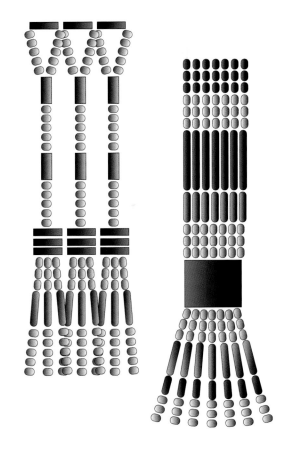

Two possible fringes for bookmarks.

TASSEL NECKS

Most tassels have a neck. Sometimes that is all they do have, no head and no skirt either. Beaded tassel necks are often tubes, made either as a flat piece of beading stitched into a cylinder or tubular beading worked on a supporting rod. These cylinders and tubes are supported by having hanks of yarn pulled through them, fitting very tightly so you often don't need to wrap the neck with another yarn.

Beads are so beautiful that a cylinder of plain beading is often all you want, but you can mix colors randomly or following any of the charts for color mixing on page 16. More pattern variations are shown below. Once you have worked out how many beads are needed for the neck of the tassel you are making, a chart can be followed for a highly patterned neck. The samples shown opposite can be worked with different colored backgrounds or changed by placing the colors in different parts of the pattern.

Simply stitched necks using either brick or peyote stitch can have added texture by using two- or three-drop versions of the stitches or by combining beads of different textures but the same color. More texture can be made by stitching beads on top, either in rows or clusters, or in loops or small dangles.

Netting is another stitch to use for covering tassel necks. More interest can be added by incorporating larger beads, cubes, or triangles, or even drops or fancy beads.

Flat and tubular beading to use for tassel necks.

Tube tassels

Simple and elegant, these small tassels are worked as a flat strip and "zipped" together to make a tube around a yarn tassel. Any bead can be used: cylinders, seeds, hexes, or charlottes—all in any size. They can be used alone or as an overskirt around a much larger tassel.

The tassels can be made using either peyote or brick stitch, whichever you prefer, but here I am giving the instructions for peyote, using size 11 beads. Any of the patterns given in the chapter on color will do for these tassels; anything more complex just isn't suitable.

Cylinder beads 3.3 (mm) size can also be used, and 2-drop peyote stitch, which looks then like a weaving pattern.

Materials
fine cord, about 10 inches long
yarn for the tassel
beads

Method
For the smallest tassel: Pick up 12 beads and work peyote stitch until you can count 12 beads along each edge. Position the edges together to make a cylinder, and sew up.

Wrap yarn around a skirt board or piece of card until you guess that there is enough to make a tassel. The skirt should be about three times as long as the cylinder, or even longer.

Knot the two ends of the cord together. Cut the yarn along one edge of the board and fold the hank over the knot. Poke the folded end of the cord through the bead cylinder. It should be a very tight fit, otherwise the beading will slide off the tassel. If it is loose, add more lengths of yarn.

Trim the bottom of the skirt.

LARGER TASSELS
For the larger tassels, use:
12 beads, count 18 on each edge
18 beads, count 18 on each edge
24 beads, count 12 on each edge
24 beads, count 18 on each edge
24 beads, count 24 on each edge.

A collection of tassels made using size 11 and 3.3 cylinder beads and mixing colors.

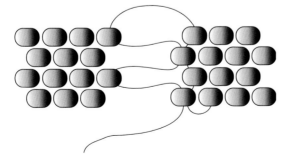

Joining flat beading to make tube tassels.

HUMBUGS

These little tassels are fun—soft because the beaded shapes are stuffed with wool, and just right as a finishing touch to a pincushion or small herb cushion. If you use cylinder beads, the tassels come out quite tiny. Seed beads make a larger size, but either type of bead works perfectly well. You will be using an even-number tubular peyote stitch.

Materials

seed or cylinder beads in 2 or 3 colors
smooth, round pencil in a plain color
dowel or rod measuring about 1½inches
    (4 cm) around the circumference
chunky knitting wool for stuffing humbugs

Method

Make 1 large humbug using the larger-diameter stick. Pick up 30 beads on the needle, make a ring by going through the beads again, and tie both ends of the thread tightly. Secure the non-working end of the thread with an elastic band, and continue working tubular peyote stitch for 20 rounds (10 beads deep). If using seed beads, you might need 2 to 4 beads less, and 2 to 4 rounds fewer, depending on their shape.

Make 9 small humbugs using a pencil with 18 to 20 beads wrapped and tied, working 12 to 14 rounds (6 beads deep). Perhaps 11 rounds, if using seed beads.

To assemble: Sew across one opening, fitting the beads together like the teeth of a zipper. Then thread on 10 beads for a hanging loop, taking the thread through twice for strength.

Stuff humbugs with short lengths of chunky wool yarn (2 wraps of yarn around your forefinger for small ones, and 5 or 6

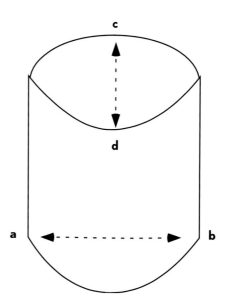

Sewing the tube from north to south, then folding it the other way
to sew it from east to west to make a humbug.

wraps for the larger one) and sew up the second opening at right angles to the first to make the humbug shape.

Thread beads onto one corner of each of the small humbugs, and sew three of them to each corner of the large humbug (but not onto the fourth corner with the loop on it). Try threading 10 beads onto one humbug, 20 onto the second, and 30 onto the third so they hang at different lengths from each corner.

WORKING SPIRAL PATTERN ON LARGE HUMBUG
Use 30 beads, threading them on in two colors (2 + 4) repeated 5 times. If using a different stick, or different beads, thread them on in multiples of 6.

Work 20 rounds, or fewer if using seed beads. Add loop as before. Sew up so that the stripes continue without a break across the seam. Stuff the humbugs as before.

USING DIFFERENT-SIZED STICKS
Tie on an even number of beads so that they fit exactly around the rod or dowel. Calculate two-thirds of the number of beads and work that many rounds: e.g., 36 beads and 24 rounds, or 42 beads and 28 rounds. You will need fewer rows if you are using seed beads.

Humbugs (2¼ and 3 inches).

FRILLED NECKS

Frills can be added to the top and bottom of a tassel neck, or in rows all the way down. Try either a netting frill or a peyote frill; they are interchangeable and look much the same, so choose whichever you prefer to do.

The tassel necks are worked on rods and the beaded frills are added after the basic neck is made. The yarn tassels are pulled through them afterwards and then decoration is added to the skirts.

Materials
Dowel rod or pencil
Seed or cylinder beads—choose a different color for the spot bead

Method (basic neck)
Using a dowel rod or pencil as a support, thread enough beads to go around the rod; the number must be divisible by four. Try 24 or 28 for a reasonable-size neck. You may have to search for a rod the correct size.

Work as many rows of tubular single peyote stitch as you wish for the depth of the neck.

YELLOW-TASSEL NECK
These frills are all the same size and are made by working two rows of 3-bead net into every third row of the peyote stitch. The second row of netting is worked into the first row, not into the neck.

BLUE NECK
This is also worked using 3-bead netting, but the rows are worked in pairs.
1. The top two rows are only one row of netting worked into alternate beads of the peyote.
2. The next two rows have a second row worked into the first one.
3. The next two rows have three rows of netting worked into the base row.
4. The bottom row has four rows of net.

This way of working gives a flared shape to the neck, which is emphasized by the narrow wrapped neck underneath.

Two frilled necks: a yellow one with frills the same size and a blue one with frills getting larger towards the base of the neck.

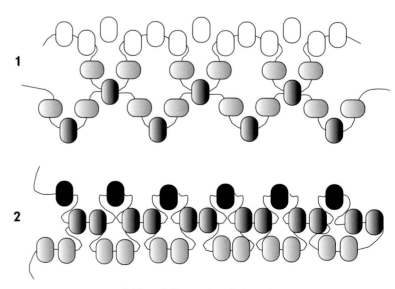

Adding frills to a beaded neck.

NETTED NECKS

These tassel necks are worked on rods and the yarn tassel is pulled through them afterwards because this gives you a neater result than if you worked them on a tassel already made.

The peyote sections at the top and bottom help the neck to grip firmly, but you can work necks entirely in horizontal netting if you wish.

Materials

dowel rod or pencil
seed or cylinder beads (larger round or cylinder beads, tiny drops, or other beads can also be used)

Method

The method for netted necks begins the same way as for frilled necks. Using a dowel rod or pencil as a support, thread enough beads to go around the rod; the number must be divisible by four. Try 24 or 28 beads for a reasonable-sized neck. You may have to search for a rod the correct size.

Work 10 rows of tubular peyote stitch, then 3 or 5 rows of 5-bead tubular net, then another 10 rows of tubular peyote stitch. This can also be varied to give more texture, with larger beads included in the netting, or extra beads added by stitching them on afterwards.

A deeper neck has 10 rows of peyote stitch, then 15 rows of 5-bead net, then 10 rows of peyote again. The spot beads can be tiny drops, petal beads, larger round beads, coiled wire beads or small blackberries.

Tassel with a frill at the top and bottom of the beaded neck (Jane Forbes).

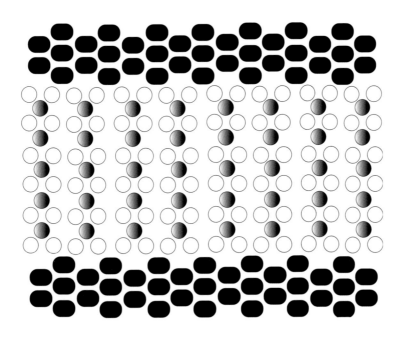

Attaching netting to the peyote strip.

PATTERNED NECKS

Charts for patterns can be hand-drawn using felt-tip pens or colored pencils on peyote or brick stitch graph papers, or more easily on the computer using one of the beading programs. These programs will also let you switch from color charts to symbols, which are sometimes easier to read.

The colors you use do not have to represent the actual colors of the beads but do have to be different from each other; otherwise, they will blend too well on the chart and make it difficult to follow. It is worth trying different-colored backgrounds in the pattern or swapping the colors in different areas within the pattern.

The chart on the right is a pattern with multiples of 8 beads, so the neck can be 24, 32, 40, or 48 beads. The neck shown in the photograph opposite is made using 48 cylinder beads, 24 in each round.

A patterned neck like this one can be made up into a tassel very simply by pulling a cord and a hank of yarn up through it and attaching a simple skirt made of narrow braids or a simple fringe.

A number of suggestions for variations on netted necks. The top of each rod shows the base and the rest have larger beads or loops attached to them or worked into the netting as you go.

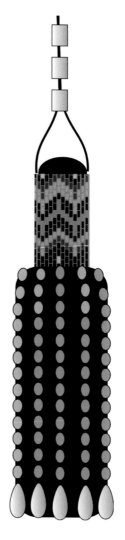

Suggestion for the finished tassel.

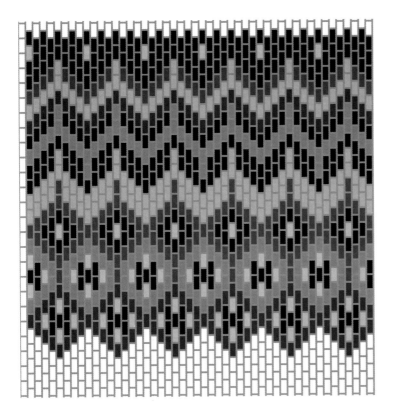

Charts colored in felt-tip pen
and designed on the computer
with the neck worked from them.
An alternative color scheme
is shown flat.

A computer color chart and black-and-white charts of the same pattern.
The change of chart proportion makes no difference in the beading.

TASSEL SKIRTS

Most tassels have skirts. These can be made entirely of yarn, of yarn with a beaded overskirt, or entirely of beading. The beading can be a fringe, or a bead fabric made with netting or any other bead stitch, depending on whether you want solid or more open beading. I have not included square stitch or right-angle weave in this book, but an open version of either of these stitches would make lovely tassel skirts.

The simplest skirts are made from a hank of yarn pulled through one or more beads, a tube of beading (which becomes the neck), or a wooden tassel mold. Fuller skirts are made by stitching yarn on a skirt board and wrapping it around the neck of a wooden mold, or by using layers of beaded skirts attached to a beaded neck or a wooden mold. The shape can be entirely controlled by the number of beads used, and can be straight, a smooth flare or A-line, or with more rounded shoulders. All sorts of decoration can be included in the beading or added afterwards. Net skirts can be given texture with beads sewn in, have short lengths or loops of beads hanging from the intersections, or be hooked up with rings or chains of beading.

The instructions given will produce the tassels in the pictures if the same beads are used, but endless variations are made simply by choosing a slightly different bead or combination of beads. If you wish to include larger beads in the netted skirts, add them to the last row of netting before the increase row. For example, work 4 rows of 5-bead netting and add larger beads as the spot beads on the fifth row. Then increase to a 7-bead netting.

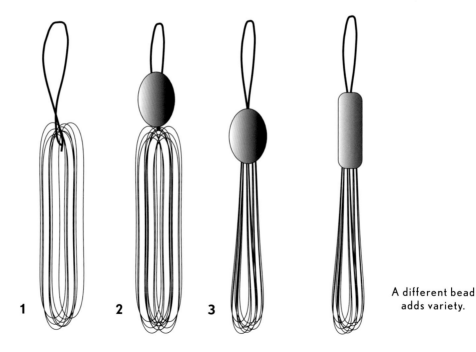

Hanks of yarn are pulled through beads to make simple tassels.

1   **2**   **3**

A different bead adds variety.

STITCHED SKIRTS

Yarn skirts are usually attached to wooden molds with flanges, using wire; but I prefer stitching. It is softer and does not necessarily need to be hidden by a ruff because it looks nice and tidy at the neck. Stitched skirts have a lovely fullness at the top, and the wooden flange bulks them out, therefore needing less yarn.

You can use a wooden skirt board for making a stitched skirt, but two pieces of thick card glued together can substitute. The skirt should be at least twice the depth of the tassel head, and can be even longer.

Use four or five fine yarns together and wind them into a ball or on a large bobbin. Fold a cord in half and knot all the ends together. Pull the fold of the cord through the tassel head with a sling. Wipe some PVA glue on the top of the knot and pull it just inside the hole at the bottom of the mold. Leave to dry.

Trim the cord and wipe some more PVA glue over the cut ends. Let dry.

Method

Tape the ends of the yarns to the bottom edge of the skirt board and then wrap them once around the board. Next, tape a strong thread in a different color along the top edge of the skirt board, leaving a tail at each end. This is called the holding thread.

Take strong button thread in a color that tones with the yarns and, leaving a short tail, knot it tightly around the wrapped yarns. Put a blunt sewing needle on the other end. Wrap the yarns around the skirt board from back to front, one wrap at a time, and stitch them to-gether with the button thread along the top edge, using simple chain stitch.

Take the first stitch over two wraps of yarns and the holding thread, and a sec-

The stages of making a stitched skirt: with the yarn wrapped and stitched on a skirt board, removed from the skirt board, the cord pulled through a painted tassel mold, and the skirt tied around the neck of the tassel mold ready for the beading.

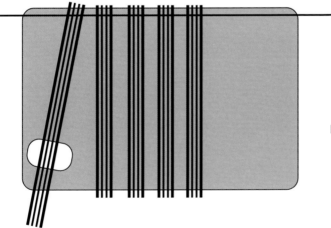

Wrap yarn around a skirt board, ready for stitching.

ond stitch on top of it. Wrap the yarns around again. Take a stitch through half the previous wrap and the whole of the current wrap, and then work another stitch on top of it. Always pull the stitches as tight as you can. You will feel slightly awkward at first, and may find that if you wrap the yarns the other way round, it suits you better. Everything becomes easier with practice.

Measure the size of the neck, using a piece of yarn. When you think the skirt is wide enough to go around the tassel neck once or twice (depending on how thick your yarns are), carefully remove all the tapes and slide the skirt off the board. Take one end of the holding thread in each hand and wind it once around the neck. The ends of the stitched skirt should meet, so pull them out or gather them in if they do not. Securely knot the ends of the holding thread together.

If you are not sure that your stitching will hold the threads, turn the tassel upside down and run a thin thread of PVA glue around the neck just under the stitching.

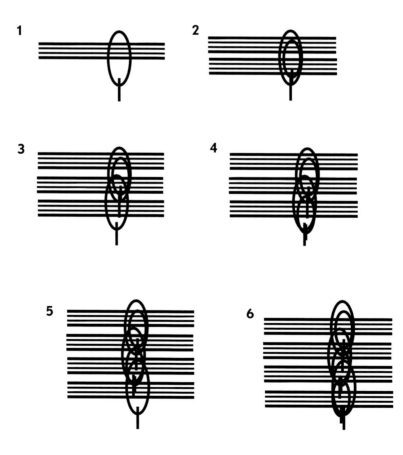

Stitching the skirt-boarded yarn using chain stitch on top of chain stitch for security.

NETTED SKIRTS

Horizontal bead netting makes lovely tassel skirts, and can be most easily attached to the base row of a peyote stitch neck worked on a supporting rod. They swing beautifully, can be patterned or in diagonal stripes, and can include larger accent beads on certain rows. The netting can be the full length of the skirt, or can reach only half or a third of the way down and be finished with a fringe hanging from the points of the netting.

The skirt shape is determined by the number of beads in the first row of netting, and also whether you hang it from every down bead at the base of the neck or into alternate downers. Netting is so similar to peyote stitch that the transition from one stitch to the other is easy.

Sometimes straight skirts can be effective if the tassel is a small one, but a flared skirt usually hangs better.

Method

Flared shape: Take the needle through one down bead at the bottom of the neck, pick up 5 beads, skip a downer and go through the next downer. The loop of beads must be slightly too long for the space between the downers, so use more beads if it is not; otherwise, the skirt will be too tight.

Work 5 rows of netting, counting the

Some of the different shapes possible in netted skirts.

This tassel uses the "gathered" skirt, padded with a ring of yarn to give smooth "shoulders" rather than folds. It is decorated with flat braids and spiral beading.

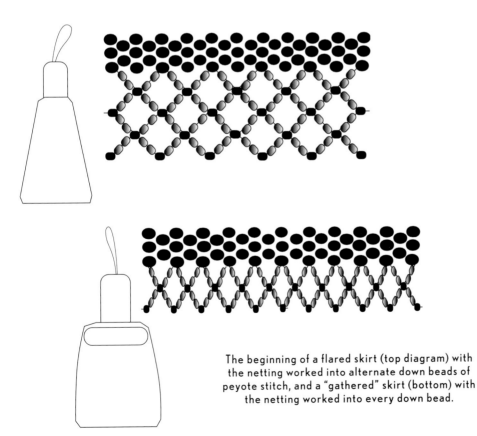

The beginning of a flared skirt (top diagram) with the netting worked into alternate down beads of peyote stitch, and a "gathered" skirt (bottom) with the netting worked into every down bead.

holes on the diagonal. Change to a 7-bead net and work 5 more rows. Change to a 9-bead net and work 5 more rows.

Continue like this until you reach the bottom of the skirt, changing to a larger-size net every fifth row.

Gathered shape: Take the needle through one down bead, pick up 5 beads, and go through the next downer. The loops of beads will stick out at first but they will sort themselves out as you work down the skirt.

If you wish to make the skirt shape smoother, you can pad the shoulders with a thick buttonhole-stitched ring of yarn, made before you start the skirt.

Netting patterns of 5 and 6 beads.

PETTICOATS

Even if a beaded tassel skirt has a yarn skirt underneath, it can look thin if there is only one layer. I like at least two layers of beading, and if there is no yarn skirt, three (or more) are not too many. Keep the underskirts, or petticoats, a plain color to show off the top layer; and if they are of different lengths, each one should be attached farther down the skirt, so the fullness will all be at the bottom and will not take too long to do.

Method

First make a beaded net underskirt, not too full, using a 5-bead net. Attach it to the base row of the neck, using alternate down beads. This is the bottom layer.

Start another layer about an inch down from the top, using a 7-bead net, and attached to the underskirt. Then make the top skirt, attaching it to the bottom row of the neck using the empty beads and a 9-bead net pattern.

If you wish to have more layers, start the second layer a couple of inches up from the bottom of the underskirt, then a second layer an inch above that and a third layer an inch above that. Each petticoat uses a larger-sized net, starting with a 5-bead, then 7-bead, then 9-bead, and so on, so that each layer fits comfortably over the previous ones.

Layers of netted skirts and petticoats.

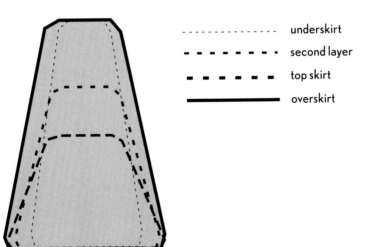

- - - - - - - - - - - - underskirt
- - - - - - - - second layer
- - - - - - top skirt
—————— overskirt

Different lengths of petticoat
attached to the underskirt.

PEACOCK TASSEL

These could be the first beaded tassels to make, using peyote stitch (or brick stitch if you prefer) for the neck and a straight 5-bead netted skirt, and using large beads as the spot beads and a yarn inner tassel.

Keep the tassel small, because the straight skirt can develop a rather odd shape if it's too long. This is an ideal tassel to hang on a pair of scissors or a key.

The large spot bead on the netted skirt can be a large round bead, a cube, a 3.3 cylinder, a triangular bead, or any novelty bead you like, provided you have enough of them. You should use a seed bead next to the large bead rather than a cylinder bead, which tends to slip inside the hole.

Materials
160 size 11 cylinder beads for the neck
320 size 11 seed beads for the skirt (or 160 seed beads and 160 cylinder beads)
80 large beads or 160 smaller beads

Method
Neck: Pick up 20 cylinder beads and take the thread through all the beads again, making a ring. Slide the beads onto a pencil and tie the two ends together in a knot. Wind the tail of the thread around the pencil above the beads, and secure it with an elastic band.

Work tubular peyote stitch for 16 rounds, counting 8 in each vertical row.

Skirt: For the netting, pick up 5 beads following the chart, skip a down bead, and take the needle through the next down bead. Repeat 4 times, finishing through the same down bead you started in. Work 16 rounds of netting and finish off the thread.

Unwind the thread from the top of the pencil and use it to add a trim on the top edge of the tassel, following the diagram. (You can also leave the top plain.) Make a cord and yarn tassel (see page 20) and pull it through the beaded neck.

Peacock tassels (2½ inches) using cube and large cylinders as the spot beads, and one with extra beads sewn into the spot beads for texture.

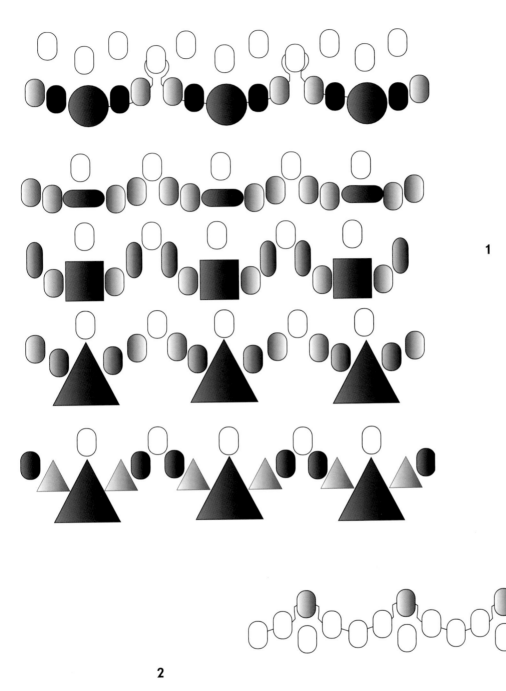

1

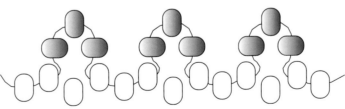

2

1. Diagrams of patterns for peacock tassel skirts, and
2. Picot edges for the tops of the necks.

FLARED-SKIRT BEADED TASSEL

These simple-to-make tassels have a plain tubular peyote- or brick-stitched neck with a two-layered netted skirt for richness. You can decorate the bottom of the skirt any way you like, with a fringe or just heavier beads sewn to the bottom points of the netting. The yarn tassel is pulled up through the beading to add bulk. You can use any yarn for this, since it does not show and is controlled by the beaded skirt.

Materials

seed or cylinder beads, mainly one color but with different-colored spot beads for the netting (more of the second color if you wish to do a spiral pattern around the neck)
larger beads for the base of the skirt
yarn for the tassel

Method

Neck: Thread on enough beads to go around a pencil, stick, or other support. The number of beads must be divisible by 4. Take the thread through the beads again to make a circle. Pull the thread tightly and knot securely, leaving at least 20 inches (½ m) of thread to work the picot and finish off. Wind the thread around the pencil and secure with an elastic band.

Work tubular peyote stitch until the neck is the desired length, at least ½ inch (2.25 cm) as it will not grip the tassel securely enough if it is any shorter.

For spiral pattern on neck: Thread beads (2 in color A and 2 in color B) until there are enough beads, which must be divisible by 4—try 16 or 20. Tie thread tightly.

Take needle through first 2 beads A, pick up the 1A bead, skip 1B, go through 2B and pull thread tight.

Pick up the 1B bead, skip the 1A bead and go through 2A and pull thread tight. At the end of the round, take the needle through the 1A bead, then the first bead of the second row, pick up the 1A bead, go through 1B, then pick up the 1B bead and go through 1A.

Continue to the end of the row, then go through the first bead of the third row.
Picot edging: Using the thread wound around the pencil, work a 3-bead picot between alternate upper beads on the top edge.
Underskirt or petticoat: Using a beading needle, work 5 rows of 6-bead netting into alternate lower beads, keeping the 2 center spot beads a different color. Work 5 rows of 8-bead netting, then 5 rows of 10-bead netting, then 2 rows of 12-bead netting.
Overskirt: Start overskirt with an 8-bead netting worked into the base row of the neck, using the alternate beads that were not used for the skirt. Work 5 rows, then 5 rows of 10-bead netting, then 5 rows of 12-bead netting. This should be shorter than the skirt.
Fringe: Add large beads to the points of the skirt and the overskirt, to add weight. You can use blackberries or wired beads instead, or add a twisted bead fringe.

MAKING UP THE TASSEL

Make a cord and knot the cut ends together. Wrap enough yarn to make the tassel and loop the cut lengths of yarn over the knot of the cord.

Comb the skirt and pull the tassel up through the beaded neck. It must fit very tightly, so add or take away more strands from the skirt if necessary. It is difficult to judge the size the first time. Trim the bottom edge.

EXTRA DECORATION

Blackberries, wired beads, or buried bugles can be sewn on at the base of the neck. Or you can work three rows of picots to simulate a ruff.

Single beads can be sewn on the cord, or threaded beads pulled through and wrapped around it.

Beaded tassels with flared skirts
(4½ and 5½ inches).
(Left tassel by Jill Carter.)

Beaded flared skirts,
ready for tasseling.

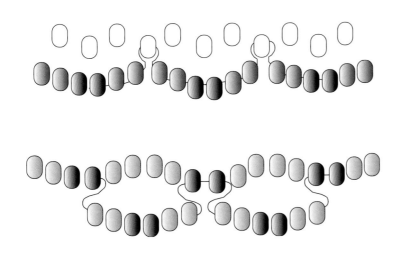

Diagram of 6-bead netting used for the top of the skirt.

PAGODA TASSELS

An attempt at trying a variation on the peacock tassels produced these pagoda tassels, with groups of 6 shallow skirts worked on a long tube of beads.

Materials
cylinder beads in 3, 4, or 5 colors, one
   color predominating
drops or fancy beads for the skirt
a wooden rod or skewer

Method
Neck: To make the narrow tube, pick up 8 or 10 of the cylinder beads and take the thread through all the beads again, making a ring. Using only 8 beads will give you a narrower skirt and 10 beads a wider one, but it really depends on which number fits your skewer.

Slide the beads onto the wooden rod and tie the two ends of the thread together in a knot. Wind the tail of the thread around the skewer above the beads and secure it with an elastic band.

Work peyote stitch for 20 rounds in color A, counting 10 in each vertical row. *Work next round in color B. Work next 3 rounds in color A.* Repeat these four rows five times. These rows mark where the skirts will be.

Work 30 rounds in color A, counting 15 in each vertical round. Repeat from * to *. Work two rounds in color A.

If you wish to have three sets of skirts, repeat the sequence one more time.

Skirts: For each small skirt, work a two-color 3-bead net into every alternate bead, starting with the bottom row on the beaded tube in color B. Then work a 5-bead net in the next round, followed by a 7-bead netting in the third round and a 9-bead net in the fourth.

Work five more skirts the same way, using the color B beads. Make each skirt a different color, or alternate the colors, or use three colors—whichever you prefer and depending on what beads you have.

Work one or two more groups of skirts the same way, using the color B beads on the tube as markers.

MAKING UP THE TASSEL
Unwind the thread from the top of the skewer. Make a fine cord, knot it at the bottom, and pull the loop through the beaded neck with a sling. Sew the beaded neck to the cord at the top to secure it, and finish off the thread. Trim the knotted cord and dab it with a bit of glue.

VARIATION
For a more cup-shaped skirt, start with 2 rows of a 5-bead net and then work 5 rows of a 7-bead net.

DECORATION
You can alter the shape of the skirt by the weight of the dangle that you add to the points on the skirts. The triple-skirted tassel with the picots and tiny gold-plated stars show the original shape because the stars weigh practically nothing.

Pagoda tassels
(3½ to 5 inches).

The smaller tassel with the black drops, which are much heavier, is a different shape. The tassel with two sets of skirts has longer fringes attached to the points, which make a different shape again.

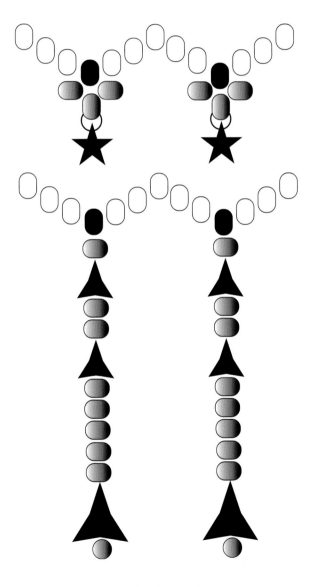

Patterns for the skirt fringes.

Chart for the neck.

CONTROLLING FLYAWAY SKIRTS

Vertical netting is extremely useful for controlling yarn skirts that are too fluffy or just the wrong shape, and any fringe would get caught up in it. Horizontal netting would be too stiff, but vertical netting is more flexible horizontally and keeps the yarn skirt nice and narrow. You can add any decoration or fringe that you wish over the top, and it will hang freely as it should do.

This netting can be made in the hand, joined in a tube, pulled over the skirt, gathered and stitched to the neck, or made as a straight piece, wrapped around the skirt, joined together, and then gathered in to the neck.

Method

String the number of beads that you will need for the length of the skirt. If you are going to work a 9-bead net, the number of beads must be divisible by 9, plus 5 beads. If you are going to work a 7-bead net, the number of beads must be divisible by 7, plus 4 beads. The spot beads can be a different color or texture.

Follow one of the diagrams until you have a piece of netting long enough to go around the yarn skirt, working an odd number of rows. Join it into a tube.

Take a thread through the topmost bead of each diamond and go through them again in a ring.

Pull the yarn skirt through the tube, and pull up the thread at the top to gather the beads into the neck of the tassel.

Tassels with vertical netting skirts controlling the yarn. (The blue-green tassel is by Jane Forbes.)

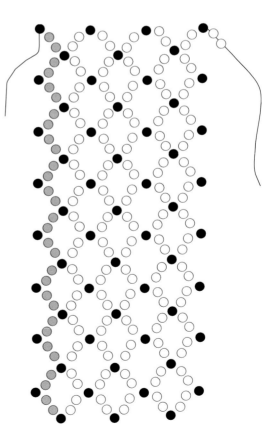

Vertical netting hung on a strong thread to tie around the neck of the tassel.

SHEPHERDESS TASSELS

Using two- and three-drop peyote stitch as a method of increasing and also shaping the skirt, make a solid skirt that sways gently from side to side in the fashion of the eighteenth-century skirts of fashionable ladies.

Materials
cylinder or seed beads
a wooden rod

Method
Neck: To make the narrow tube, pick up an even number of beads to fit around the rod and take the thread through all the beads again, making a ring.

Slide the beads onto the rod and tie the two ends of the thread together in a knot. Wind the tail of the thread around the rod above the beads and secure it with an elastic band.

Work single peyote stitch for about 20 rounds, counting 10 in each vertical row.
Skirt: Work 2 rows of two-drop peyote in the plain color. This will bunch up as you work, but don't worry. It will come right as you go on.

Change to three-drop peyote and work as many rows as you wish for the skirt.

MAKING UP THE TASSEL
Unwind the thread from the top of the skewer and finish it off. Make a fine cord and knot the two ends together. Wrap yarn around a skirt board or wire frame. You must guess at the number of times, but more can be added later on if there is not enough.

Cut the yarn and loop the hank through the cord just above the knot. Pull the cord and yarn up through the skirt and neck of the tassel, until the yarn just shows at the top.

The hank of yarn must fit into the neck tightly. If the yarn skirt is longer than the beaded skirt, trim it.

DECORATION
A row of picots can be added to the top of the neck and the bottom edge of the skirt, and you can hang a larger drop bead from the bottom row of picots. The green tassel in the picture has long strips of 2-bead braid knotted in the center, and stitched to the base of the neck.

VARIATION
A sequence of two-drop, three-drop, and five-drop peyote stitch makes a larger tassel (the white one in the photo above) with a layered skirt.

Shepherdess tassels using single, three-drop, and five-drop peyote stitch. The finished tassel is decorated with knotted strips of a 2-bead flat braid.

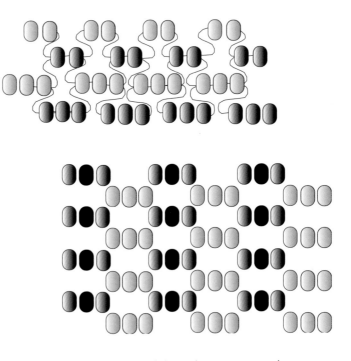

5.20 Diagrams of two- and three-drop peyote stitch.

FRINGES

Almost anything looks better with a fringe on it, which gives the movement and sparkle that is so characteristic of beads. Fringes can be added to the bottoms of tiny bags or bookmarks, used as a necklace, or added to the bottom edge of a lampshade. Couture clothes often have fringes on them: on the yoke, on the edge of a jacket, or all over a dress. A tassel can have an overskirt of a fringe, or the whole skirt can be layers of fringes, perhaps all of different lengths.

Although most of the beading stitches in this book need *even* beads with quite large holes, you can use all your *uneven* beads with small holes in the fringe, as well as larger beads from old necklaces, homemade paper or wire beads, or really expensive accent beads that you can only afford a few of.

Straight fringes are the easiest to make, with the strings all the same length. However, the bottom edge of a fringe can be any shape, and the diagrams here show how varied it can be.

ATTACHING FRINGE

A fringe can be attached to the edge of any beading, using a slightly different method in each case.

Opposite, the lower diagrams show how to attach a fringe to:
1. peyote stitch—each string hung onto each down bead along the edge;
2. brick stitch—going up through a bead and down through the next bead between each string; but hooking a string of beads onto the loops of thread on the edge of brick stitch is not a good idea because the thread might break;
3. the points on netting.

Other ways to attach fringe will be explained later.

A bead fringe incorporating tiny cylinder beads worked on a
bead braid woven on a tiny inkle loom.

Simple fringes on tiny bags. The fringes on the bronze-and-black and gold-and-gray bags are stitched to the brick-stitch base. The fringe on the blue-and-frosted bag is worked in three layers.

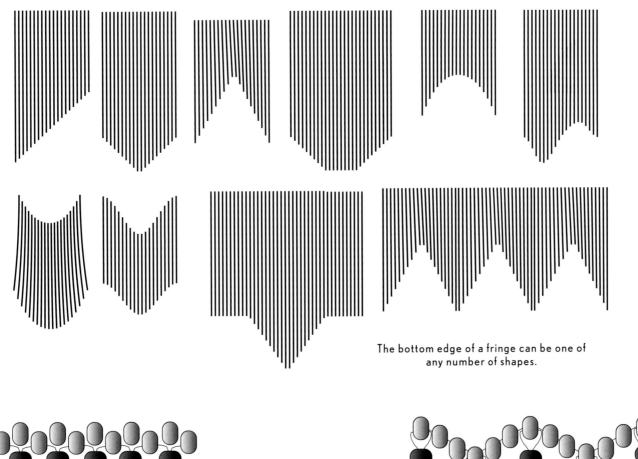

The bottom edge of a fringe can be one of any number of shapes.

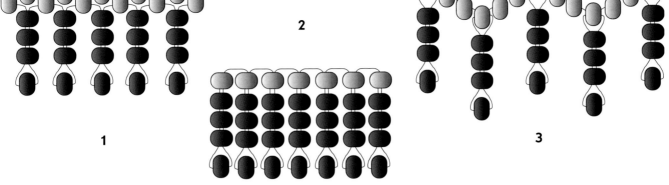

Attaching a simple fringe to peyote stitch, brick stitch, and netting.

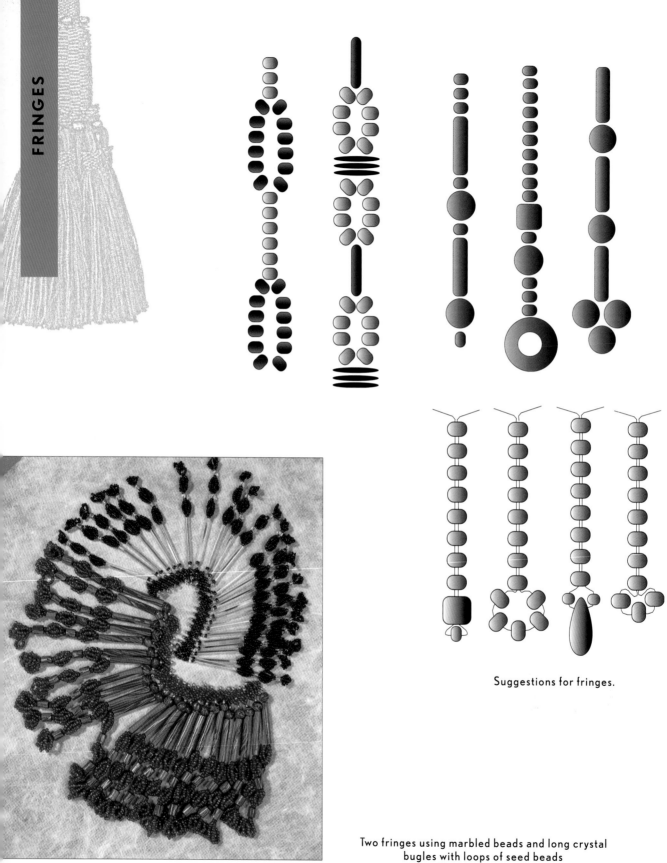

Suggestions for fringes.

Two fringes using marbled beads and long crystal
bugles with loops of seed beads
(Lynn Horniblow).

BEADED OVERSKIRT

You can add a beaded overskirt to a yarn tassel, which need not be too dense and can use a variety of different beads, or you can make an entirely beaded skirt, in which case it should be quite dense, or even made in two layers.

Method

String an even number of beads long enough to go around the neck of the mold. Go through the beads again to make a loose ring, and slip over the flange at the bottom of the mold. Pull both ends of the thread tight and tie them together.

Add a fringe, using any of the previous patterns, going through either every bead around the neck or around every alternate bead for a more open skirt. Do this by taking the needle through a bead on the neck, picking up as many beads as you wish for the string of the fringe; skip the bottom bead, and take the needle back up through the string and then horizontally through the next bead on the neck.

If you wish to make two layers of fringe, string another length of beads and make another ring that sits on the neck above the first one. Add strings of beads or the fringe as before. This second layer can hang straight down, mingling with the first layer, or it can be draped and swagged over the top.

You may wish to add a ruff to the neck to finish it off.

Curtain tie-back using an enormous mixture of beads leftover from old necklaces. The fringe is made on a flat braid which just fits around the neck of the mold (Jane Forbes).

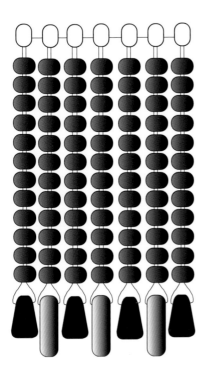

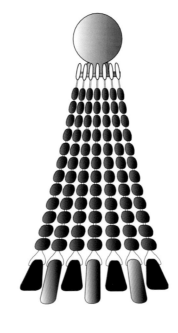

A beaded fringe attached to a string of beads to tie around the neck of a mold.

BRANCHED FRINGE

These fringes are bulkier than straight fringes, and can look like the roots of a tree. The only historical examples I can find are those made in Afghanistan, which are illustrated here.

The tension should be kept very tight so that the branches stick out sideways from the main stem.

Method

Use either a beaded strip or braid, or a string of beads, as a base and bring your needle out through a bead at the end. Thread enough beads for the whole length of the stem. Skip the end bead and then take the needle up and through only a few beads.

Add on a few more beads, skip the end bead, and take the needle back up through the few beads you have just added on. Pull the thread tight.

Take the needle through a few more beads on the stem and bring the needle out, ready to pick up a few more beads for the next branch.

The branches will stick out on both sides as they feel like it, but you can adjust them when you have finished the fringe.

RING FRINGE

This is a variation on the branched fringe, made by picking up a few beads for the ring; but instead of going back up through them, take the needle into the main stem, making a loop, and go through a few more beads before making another ring.

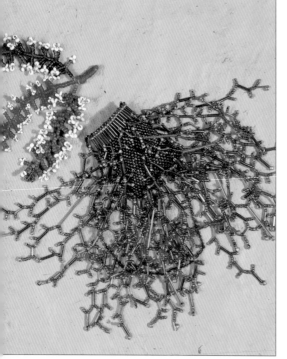

A bag and an Afghanistan tassel using branched fringes.

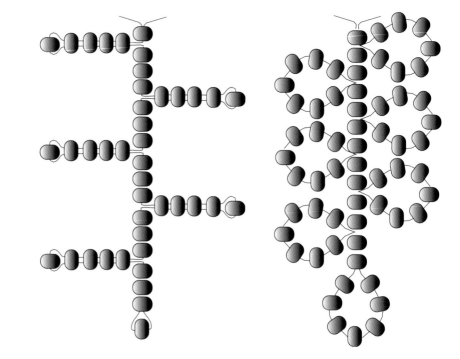

Diagrams for a branched fringe and a ring fringe.

Y FRINGES

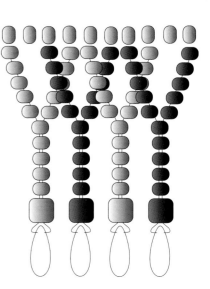

A Y fringe.

These fringes look slightly different from straight fringes, and rows can be overlapped, giving quite a complex pattern at the top.

Method

Use either a beaded strip or braid, or a string of beads, as a base; the number of beads on the edge must be divisible by four, or six, according to your design.

Take the needle out of one of the beads of the strip, pick enough beads for the string and, skipping the bottom bead, take the needle back through the beads nearly to the top of the string—leaving, say, six beads that you do not go through. Pick up six more beads and take the needle through a different bead four (or six) beads away.

Another row can be attached to the beads between the loops.

TWISTED FRINGE

These fringes are the most beautiful of all, always hanging well and looking really rich at the base of a bag or on a tassel.

Method

Use either a beaded strip or braid, or a string of beads, as a base and take your needle out of one of the beads to start the fringe. Pin the other end of this strip to a cork board to hold it in place while you work.

Pick up at least twice as many beads as you need for the measured length of the fringe.

Drop the needle and grab the thread near the last bead.

Lick or dampen the thumb and forefinger on both your hands and begin twisting the thread. Do *not* let go of the thread while you are twisting, and count the number of twists you do. It should be about 40 or 50, or even more for a very long fringe.

Still holding the thread by the last bead, fold the length of beads in half to see if it twists well. If it does, then, still holding the thread, take the needle back into the braid to secure the fringe.

Bring the needle down through the next bead and repeat the process, using the same number of twists.

VARIATION

A drop bead, or string of beads, can be added to the center of this fringe. To do this, stop picking up beads at the halfway point, and add the string, skipping the base bead and going back up through the string until you get to the original length of beads (as you would do for a straight fringe); then, continue to pick up enough beads for the second half.

When you pull the beads out straight to start twisting, the extra string will hang down from the center point and won't be included in the twist.

A twisted fringe worked on a braid.

LOOPED FRINGES

Looped fringes often hang better than straight ones, even when you are using cylinder beads.

Method

Use either a beaded strip or braid, or a string of beads, as a base; the number of beads on the edge must be divisible by 4, or 6, according to your design.

Take the needle out of one of the beads of the strip, pick enough beads for the loop, and take the needle back through a different bead 4 (or 6) beads away. Further rows will be attached to the beads between the loops.

If the center bead is a heavy one, the loop will hang in a V, but with beads of equal weight the loops are very regular and hang in a beautiful curve.

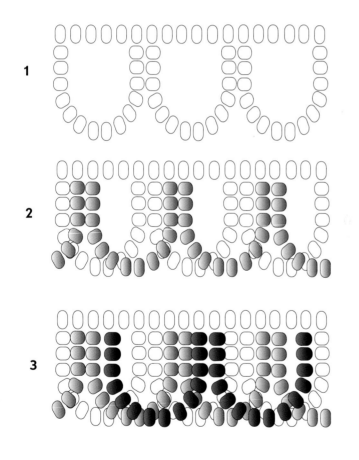

1

2

3

Stages of a three-layered looped fringe.

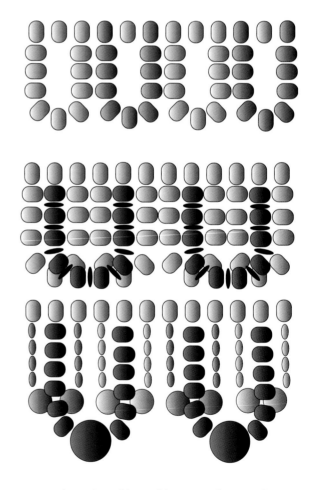

A number of looped fringes with one and two layers.

LOOP-STRIP TASSELS

These tassels are made by working a fringe, either straight or looped, into a narrow strip of beading, and then coiling it around a tassel head, or around a twisted cord for a smaller tassel.

Materials

a cord about 10 inches long
seed or cylinder beads
larger beads for the bases of the loops

Method

Work a two-bead peyote strip until it is about 4 inches long or longer. Plan a symmetrical fringe with a heavier bead or beads in the center of each loop.

To add the loops, take the thread down through the first bead on one side of the peyote strip, pick up all the beads for a single loop, and go back up through a bead in the strip. You can go into either alternate beads, or every third or fourth bead if you are going to do a double layer of loops, or every sixth bead if you are going to do three layers.

Continue until you have added all the loops, but leave the thread hanging to sew the beading to the cord.

Fold the cord in half and knot the two ends together. Sew one end of the strip of beading to the knot, covering it with the beading. Wind the strip up the cord, sewing it to the cord at intervals and at the top.

A looped fringe and a tiny bag with loops attached to the brick-stitch base.

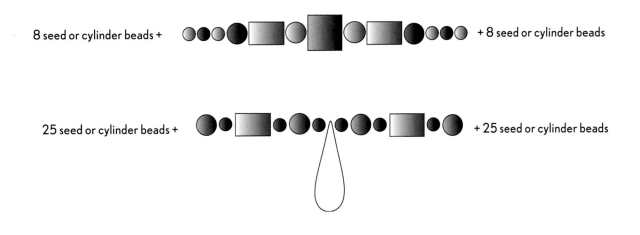

8 seed or cylinder beads +   + 8 seed or cylinder beads

25 seed or cylinder beads +   + 25 seed or cylinder beads

Patterns for the strings of two looped fringes.

SMALL GRAY TASSEL

The peyote strip is 4 beads wide and 60 beads long on each side. The length of each loop is 2 inches.

Materials

size 11 transparent gray seed beads
size 11 matte gray, rust, and black cylinder beads
size 3.3 matte silver cylinder beads
gold/rust/purple variegated shiny 4 by 4 cubes

Method

The first layer of loops is threaded through every sixth bead, and the second layer more or less in the center of each gap. Then, for each loop, thread:

(1 gray and 1 silver cylinder bead) five times
1 rust, 1 black, and 1 copper cylinder bead
1 gray seed bead, 1 gray 3.3 cylinder, 1 gray seed, 1 cube, 1 gray seed, 1 gray 3.3 cylinder and 1 gray seed
1 copper, 1 black, and 1 rust cylinder bead
(1 gray and 1 silver cylinder bead) five times

PINK, CREAM AND BRONZE TASSEL

The peyote strip is 2 beads wide and 90 beads long on each side. Each loop is 2 ½ inches long.

Materials

size 11 cylinder beads in bright pink metallic, cream, bronze, soft wine transparent, and pale pink Ceylons
size 11 seed beads in transparent soft wine
size 8 seed beads in bronze
ponies in metallic bronze

Method

The first layer of loops is threaded through every sixth bead, and the second and third rows in the beads next to them.
For each loop, thread:
5 bronze, 5 pale pink, 5 cream, and 5 bright metallic pink cylinder beads
1 size 11 seed bead, 1 size 8 seed bead, 1 pony, 1 size 8 seed bead, and 1 size 11 seed bead
5 bronze, 5 pale pink, 5 cream, and 5 bright metallic pink cylinder beads

LARGER BRONZE TASSEL

The peyote strip is 4 beads wide and 90 beads long on each side. The loops are nearly 4 inches long.

Materials

size 11 bronze and black cylinder beads
size 11 bronze cut seed beads
3.3 bronze cylinder beads
variegated shiny cubes

Method

For each loop, thread:
15 bronze cylinder beads
10 alternate black and bronze cylinder beads
(1 seed bead, 1 3.3 cylinder bead) three times
1 cube
(1 seed bead, 1 3.3 cylinder bead) three times
10 alternate black and bronze cylinder beads
15 bronze cylinder beads
The first layer of loops is threaded through every sixth bead, and the second and third rows in the beads next to them.

LONG FISH TASSEL WITH SKIRT

This tassel is made slightly differently from the others in that the fringe is coiled over the top of a Chinese tassel, made using tassel method 3.

The fringe is slightly different in that each loop of beads uses 100 seed beads, and is looped into the next bead on the base strip instead of every sixth bead.

The loops are worked in groups of four, and then a slim tassel, made using method number 1, is hung on the next bead.

Articulated metal fish decorations, available in craft stores, or any other large long beads may then be hung on 9 seed beads amongst the bead groupings.

Loop-strip tassels (3 to 3 ½ inches). The long one has extra yarn tassels between the loops and is decorated with metal fish. (The bronze-and-gold tassel is by Jacquie Tinch.)

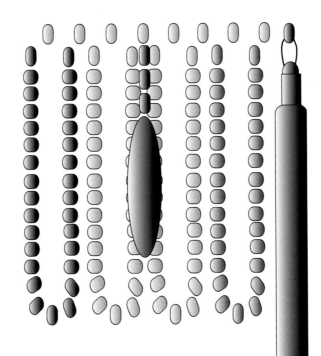

Pattern for the fringe on the fish tassel.

These tassels are full of nostalgia, reminiscent of old, beaded lampshades. The number of peyote strips can vary with the size of the mold, and so can the number of loops.

COPPER AND CREAM TASSEL
A yarn skirt gives this flamboyant tassel extra bulk.

Materials
a cord about 12 or 13 inches long
seed or cylinder beads (I used 10 colors
   in each tassel)
wooden tassel mold 2 ½ inches high and
   1 ¼ inches wide
(A different tassel mold could be used, but you will need to adjust the instructions.)

Method
Paint the wooden mold. The copper one in the photograph opposite is painted with nail polish and the silver one is marbled with metallic paint.

Knot the ends of the cord together, and glue it into the tassel mold (see page 98). Work six 4-bead peyote strips until they are about 4 inches long. (They can be adjusted as you do the looped skirt, if you leave the ends of the thread hanging at the bottom.) Finish off the thread at the top of each strip.

To attach the strips to the neck of the mold, take a newly threaded needle and go through all 4 beads at the top of a strip, pick up 2 or 3 beads (depending on the size of the neck), go through all four beads of the second strip, and pick up 2 or 3 beads. Continue until all the strips are on your thread, the picked-up beads acting as spacers between them.

Take the thread through all the beads again, making a loose ring. Slip it over the flange at the base of the mold onto the narrow neck. Knot the ends of the thread firmly.

Take the needle through the second row of beads on the nearest braid from right to left, ready to add the loops. Pick up 4 beads and go through the second row of the next braid on the left. Continue doing this until you are back at the beginning again.

Drop down one row, ready to begin the next row of loops.

The loops are shaded from the darkest to the lightest in the center and back again, using 9 colors altogether, 2 beads of each color.

For each loop, thread:
first row, 4 beads
second row, 6 beads
third row, 8 beads
fourth row, 10 beads

Continue increasing 2 beads every row until you have reached 36 beads in each loop.

Continue adding 36-bead loops until the skirt is about 4 to 5 inches long, adjusting the lengths of the braids as you need to.

Cord: Partially cover the cord with strung beads wrapped around it in the opposite direction to the twist of the cord. Thread the beads in the same sequence of colors you used for the loops on the skirt, and secure both ends of the thread by sewing into the cord itself.

Add three rows of loops following diagram 3 on page 91, each row a different number of beads.

Collar: Make a 2-bead peyote strip long enough to go around the cord where it emerges from the tassel mold; the number of beads must be divisible by 4. It does not matter if the collar is slightly loose.

Ruff: You may feel that this tassel does not need a ruff, or you could put one around the neck and another at the base of the cord. Make a 2-bead peyote strip, with 6-bead loops, following the instructions on page 103.

Fringe: Make 2 twisted fringes at the bottom of each strip, each fringe with 60 beads.

SILVER AND PINK TASSEL

This is worked on a smaller head using only 5 beaded strips around the neck. The loops are made in the same way but increase 2 in each row all the way down.

There are 8 colors in this skirt, 4 rows of each color.

Check that all the strips hang down 25 stitches on each side below the last loop.

Fold each one up on the inside of the skirt and sew firmly. Make ruff and collar as before.

Scalloped tassels (4 ½ and 7 inches).

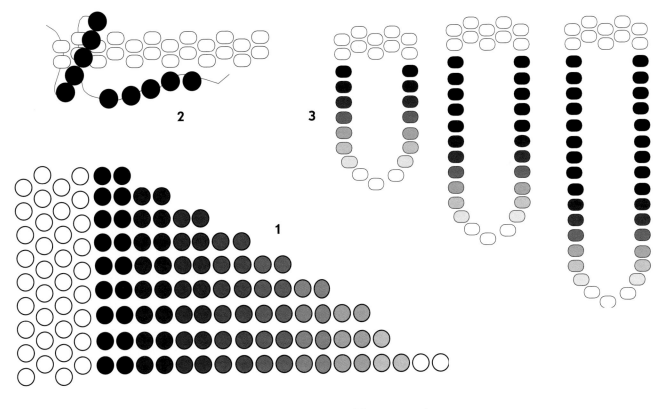

1. Color shaded towards the center for pink-and-bronze tassel.
2. Diagram of the ruff.
3. Diagram of loops worked on top of pink-and-bronze tassel head.

TASSEL HEADS

Tassels usually have heads, sometimes including wooden molds but often made from rolled-paper beads or card cylinders that previously held embroidery thread or sticky tape. Improvisation is the name of the game here, and it's worth going through your drawers and boxes to find leftover odd items that could be painted or covered with beading.

A tassel head can also be made entirely of beads, perhaps a ball of beads or other bead shapes such as cones or cubes. Pieces of beading—such as a sample you did while you were learning a stitch and have no other use for—can be folded origami-style to make a tassel head. Hang some strings of beads from it for the skirt. A foam plastic ball can be painted or totally covered with foil, and then a netting of beads added.

The simplest tassel is made from a single bead (wooden, glass, or metal) with a hank of yarn and a cord pulled through it. This is a good way to show off your single interesting bead. A hank of yarn can be pulled through a large disk and wrapped to make a neck which is then covered with a bead collar.

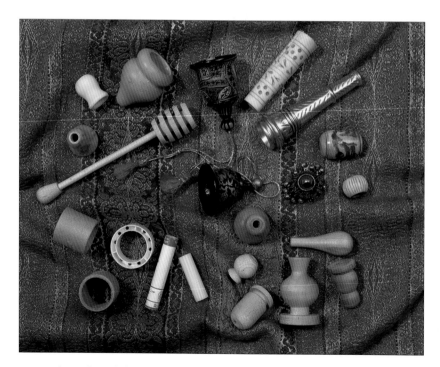

A number of things can be used for tassel heads: card and plastic cylinders, finials for curtain poles, large beads, blind pulls, a hookah mouthpiece, large carved-bone cylinders, and candle cups.

An impressive tassel made by covering a plastic inner support from a roll of cellophane tape and the cylinders inside machine embroidery thread with peyote stitch.

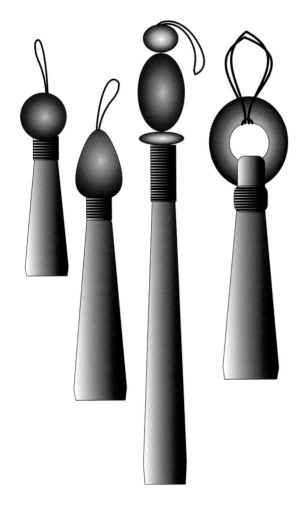

Simple tassels made by pulling a hank of yarn folded over a cord through a bead, or folded over a disk, and wrapping the neck.

LOOPED BALL TASSEL

These tassels are extremely quick and easy to make, and are a larger, looser version of the blackberries on page 111, using loops of strung beads instead of single beads.

The intertwining loops can be made using up many of your leftover beads in different sizes. Forget counting also. No matter how many times I try, I cannot count the number of loops that are needed—I get so engrossed in making the shape that the counting gets forgotten! The balls can be fairly loose, or tighter and more compact, depending on how many loops you thread through. It is nearly impossible to repeat one of these exactly, so if you are making a pair, work them both together.

These tassels can be made from cylinder or seed beads, and I like them even better when larger beads are included in the loops. The diagrams show what has been used for the tassels in the illustration—seeds, cylinders (both small and large), cubes, and drops. A couple of the tassels have been made by using flower chains and some other braids to give a more solid ball.

**Looped ball tassels
(1 to 3½ inches).**

Method

Thread on about 15 beads, then go through them again to make a ring, and tie the thread ends together. Thread on another 15 beads in a different color, and go through 3 or 4 beads somewhere on the first ring.

Continue like this, adding loops of 15 beads each time, weaving and looping in and out of the mass of beads and going through a few beads on another ring to secure them.

Roll the ball around in your fingers until you have a good shape, and keep adding loops until you are pleased with the result. If there is a hollow, put a loop in it.

Make a 13- or 15-bead ring through what you consider to be the top of the tassel to hang it by, threading the needle through the beads at least twice.

Braid loops: Make a 2-bead peyote strip that is 15 beads long on each side. Join it into a ring and tie the ends of the thread together in a knot.

Pick up 2 beads on the needle, go back through the ring and forward again and also through the 2 beads you have just added. Work a strip as before, 15 beads along each side, and join the end firmly to the other side of the original ring.

Continue adding braids, weaving in and out of previous ones, until the ball is as large as you wish. After joining the end of each strip to a previous one, weave the thread in and out so that each loop is started at a new place.

To hang the ball, make a separate 2-bead strip and link it with one of the loops on the ball before you join it into a ring.

Fringe: You do not need to add a fringe, but if you wish one, start a new thread somewhere in the center of the base of the ball, and pick up about 50 beads for each strand. Do not put too heavy a bead on the bottom of the strands or they will pull some loops out of shape.

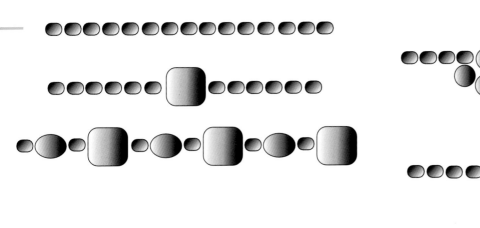

Diagrams of the strings of loops to make
the different tassels.

COILED-STRIP TASSEL

These frilled tassels are soft, do not use many beads, and are ideal for attaching to small items to identify them as your own.

They can be made in three different ways: as a strip with a frill on one edge wound around a cord, wound around the head of a simple tassel, or as a more tailored frill using a slightly different method of construction.

Materials
cord about 8 inches long
yarn for the tassel
seed or cylinder beads in one main color
small amounts of seed or cylinder beads
   in 2 or 3 other colors

Method (coiled strip on cord)
This method gives a softer frill. Using the main color, work a 4-bead strip of peyote stitch until it is about 4 inches long. To attach the frill, pick up one bead and take

the needle up through the first bead on the long edge.

Pick up another bead and take the needle up through the second bead. Continue until you have a row of beads along the edge, sitting on top of the last row of the beaded strip.

Frill: Using a different color, pick up 2 beads, and take the needle through the last bead of the previous row. Pick up 2 more beads and take the needle through the next bead. Continue until you reach the end.

Continue working two-drop peyote, picking up 2 beads and taking the needle through 2 beads, using a different color for each row. There should be 5 rows on the frill.

Coiled-strip tassels (9 inches). The braid strips with different edges are coiled neatly or at random around cords or the heads of yarn tassels.

MAKING UP THE TASSEL

Method 1 (basic)

Fold a length of cord in half and knot the two ends together. Sew one end of the strip of beading to the knot, covering it with the beading. Wind the strip up the cord in a corkscrew, sewing it to the cord at intervals and at the top.

Method 2 (coiled strip)

Work the frilled strip as in method 1, but make it up slightly differently. Fold the cord in half and knot the ends together. Wind a hank of yarn, then loop it through the cord just above the knotted ends. Fold the hank in half and wrap the neck to secure the tassel.

Sew one end of the strip of beading to the knot, covering it with the beading. Wind the strip up the cord, sewing it to the cord at intervals and at the top.

Method 3 (corkscrew)

This method gives a flatter frill and a more tailored coil, with the frill overlap-ping the flat strip of beading. Using the main color, work a 4-bead strip of peyote stitch until it is about 4 inches long. Pick up 2 beads, and take the needle down through one bead on the edge of the strip and then back up through the next bead.

Pick up 2 more beads, and take the needle down through one bead on the edge of the strip then back up through the next bead. Continue like this until you have reached the end of the strip and the beads are lying in sets of 2 along the edge.

Frill: Using a different color, pick up 2 beads and then take the needle through the last bead of the previous row.

Pick up 2 more beads and take the needle through the next bead. Continue until you reach the end of the row.

Continue working two-drop peyote, picking up 2 beads and taking the needle through 2 beads, using a different color for each row. I have used 7 rows of bead-ing on these tassels, but you could add more.

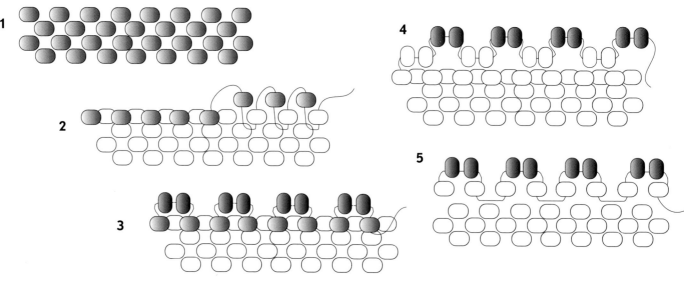

Adding a fringe to the edge of a flat braid.

WOODEN TASSEL MOLDS

With the increase in popularity of tassel making, it is getting easier to find wooden tassel molds—often from suppliers of lace equipment. Any woodturner could make them for you, if you simply draw a shape or search out an illustration of what you want. You can also find many other substitutes, such as wooden egg cups, door handles, or finials from curtain poles. These will need a hole drilled through the middle. Try using dome-shaped plastic tops from skin care bottles, again with a drilled hole. Large wooden beads and disks, window blind pulls, napkin rings, peg doll stands, tiny reels, and other shapes can be bought from large craft shops if you nose around all the different sections.

Most of these shapes can be used on their own, perhaps with beaded ruffs and a cord knotted at the top of the mold, but try combining different shapes to make even more distinctive tassels. See the illustration on page 9 for small hard tassels made from tiny reels and wooden beads, painted, with beaded collars around the straight sections.

Almost any shape is improved with a ball at the top, or a disk, or both. The diagrams show some of the possibilities, but look all through the book for other ideas. Complex combinations can include painted or gilded molds with a single beaded or rolled mold. If you can find only small molds, then putting two or three together is one way of making a larger, more important tassel, for a curtain tie-back, for example.

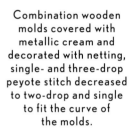

Combination wooden molds covered with metallic cream and decorated with netting, single- and three-drop peyote stitch decreased to two-drop and single to fit the curve of the molds.

Some of the possible shapes of wooden tassel molds.

Combinations of different shapes make more interesting heads.

ROLLED TASSEL MOLDS

Traditionally, gimp was most often used for rolled heads, as they are called, but you can use a finely twisted cord or a metallic embroidery thread instead. I think this method makes a lovely-looking head, but you cannot always find the right color of gimp. Making your own fine cord solves that problem, and you will need about 4 to 6 yards of either to cover a medium-sized mold (about 2 ½ to 3 inches deep). However, it always better to have more than you need because it is impossible to join gimp or cord in the middle of a mold.

Simple wooden shapes, or stout card or plastic cylinders, are the easiest to cover, but more complex shapes can be done without difficulty when you are more practiced.

Materials

wooden tassel molds
gimp, cord, or fancy thread
    wooden skewer
    glue

Method

Using the tip of a wooden skewer, put a little glue just inside the top of the hole of a wooden tassel mold. Press the first inch or so of cord against it and leave it to dry with the rest of the cord hanging down on the outside.

Put more glue around the rim of the hole and carefully arrange cord on it, making a nice circle. Let dry. Apply more glue just underneath the glued cord, using the wooden skewer, and carefully wind the cord over the glue next to the previous row. Keep winding until you reach bare wood without any glue on it.

If the shape is simple, or you are covering an outer curve (when the shape is gradually getting larger), you can do three or four rounds at a time. If it is more complex, or you are covering an inner curve (and the shape is getting smaller), you might be able to glue only half a round at a time. Press the cord up against the previous round so that there are no gaps.

When the shape is covered, put some glue on the neck of the mold and wind the end of the thread around it so that it is completely secure. Add more glue to make sure the thread will not come undone. This thread will be covered by the skirt. Leave the whole thing to dry overnight.

Tassel molds rolled with gimp and beads, or strings of beads. One string has gold leaf applied over the rolled beads.

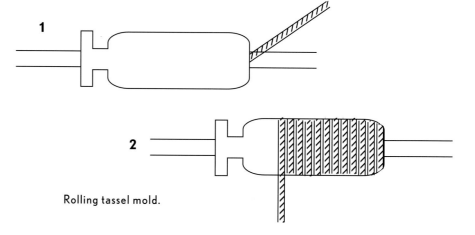

1

2

Rolling tassel mold.

ROLLED-BEAD HEADS

Threaded beads can be glued to a tassel mold in the same way as the rolled gimp heads. The beads can be all one color, or threaded in patterns, or in random mixes of color. Simple wooden shapes, or stout card or plastic cylinders, are the easiest to cover, but more complex shapes can be done without difficulty, provided only a short length of beads is glued on at the same time.

The rolled beads do make the mold much bigger, especially if you are using size 11 seed beads, so make allowances for this when choosing your mold.

You can wind the beads on clockwise or counterclockwise—whichever you find easiest. Because I am right-handed I find that rolling clockwise is the best for me.

Materials

wooden tassel molds
ready-thread beads, seed or cylinder beads

Method

Thread a large number of beads on Nymo thread, leaving the tail attached to the reel. This work is rather boring, but you need at least 2 feet of threaded beads to start. Then take the needle off the thread and tie a knot around the last bead so that it is secure. Trim the thread, leaving about an inch of tail.

Using the tip of a wooden skewer, put a little glue just inside the top of the hole of a wooden tassel mold. Press the first 2 or 3 beads against it and leave to dry, the rest of the threaded beads hanging loose on the outside. Put more glue around the rim of the hole and carefully arrange the threaded beads on it.

Pull the thread reasonably tight so there are no gaps between the beads. Let dry. Apply more glue just beneath the first beads and carefully wind the beads

over the glue next to the previous row.

As with rolled tassel molds, press the beads up against the previous round so that there are no gaps.

When you begin to run out of beads, unwind the thread attached to the reel, cut it off and thread the needle onto it. I usually reel off a couple of yards, actually meters, depending on the size of the mold, leaving plenty so that the beads do not come off accidentally.

When the shape is covered, put some glue on the neck of the mold and wind the end of the thread around it. Add more glue to make sure that the thread will not come undone. This thread will be covered by the skirt.

RANDOM COLORS

Put all your leftover beads into a small pot and stir thoroughly to mix them. If the mix looks insipid, add plenty of a dark color or gold. Four or five shades of one color are also effective. When you thread them on, make sure that you don't pick the same color twice, and that the colors are really well mixed.

PATTERNS

This method makes quite different patterns according to the shape of the mold. I like it best on a ball, but on an onion shape or a drop shape you will get one pattern at the top of the mold, a different one in the middle of the mold, and another pattern at the base!

Thread your beads in groups of the following:
10 color A, (1 color B, 1 color A) 5 times,
    10 color B, (1 color A, 1 color B). Repeat.
2 color A, 2 color B, 2 color C, etc. Repeat.
5 color A, * 1 color B, 1 color A, 5 color
    B, 1 color C, 1 color B, 5 color C, 1 color
    A, 1 color C, 5 color A. Repeat from *.

Tassels with wooden molds rolled with random and sequences of beads (tassel above by Lynn Horniblow).

NETTED TASSEL MOLDS

Many traditional tassels have a netting of buttonhole stitch over the molds. A bead netting gives a similar look, but is even more textured.

A vertical net is by far the best one to use because it is more flexible and will expand and contract to fit most simple shapes. Do not attempt to cover very intricate shapes with a net; they are best left painted.

Method

Use a mold that has been painted or rolled with gimp or metallic thread. String enough beads, following the netting diagram shown here, about ½ inch longer than the mold. This will allow for drawing the net in slightly over the top and bottom edges to secure it.

Work enough rows until the net fits around the widest part of the mold when stretched, working an odd number of rows. Join it into a cylinder, keeping the pattern accurate.

Slip the net over the mold before you finish off the thread. It must be stretched quite tightly, and if it is at all loose, undo a couple of rows.

Gather the net at the top and bottom, adding extra beads to fill the spaces if necessary. Pull the threads tightly to keep the net stretched.

Once the net is on, it can be decorated in any number of ways, similar to netted skirts.

Extra beads can be sewn on, small loops added to the spot beads, or swags and strings of beads can spiral around the netted mold.

Pattern for vertical netting.

SNAILING

Wrapping tassel molds with beaded braids so that they cross over the mold is called snailing. It looks best on a rounded mold, so the snailing stays in place better, and the mold can be rolled with gimp—which helps the braid to grip it. On other shapes you can control the snailing with tiny rings of beading where they cross over.

Use a very narrow beaded braid on small heads; it can be further decorated any way you please.

The following method is slightly different from the traditional method of snailing with a yarn cord because the beaded braids need more control to stop them from slipping.

Method

Make a ring of beads to fit around the narrow neck of the mold. Work a length of braid to fit over the mold, and attach one end to the ring of beads. Take the braid over and around the mold, and attach the other end to the ring of beads on the opposite side.

Add 3 more braids of the same length in the same fashion, starting and finishing at equidistant spacing. The braids should go over and under each other alternately.

VARIATIONS

Gimp rolled or painted heads can also be decorated with straight rows of beaded braids, attached to a ring of beads at the neck as before. At the top of the mold, where there is nothing to attach them to, the ends of the sewing thread can be taken down inside the mold, pulled out through the bottom hole, and sewn to the knot in the cord after it has been pulled through. A line of glue under the braids will keep them in place.

Wooden molds rolled with beads in set sequences to make a pattern which alters as the mold gets wider or narrower, netted molds with vertical netting worked separately and fitted to the molds, sometimes with extra beads stitched on top, and molds with snailing and added braids, tiny flowers, and strings of beads.

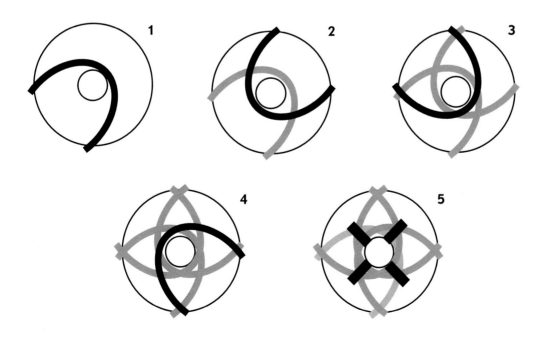

The sequences of snailing on a tassel head.

TRIMMINGS & BAUBLES

Most tassels need a trimming of some sort, and it is almost impossible to overdecorate a tassel, provided the trimmings are designed for that particular one. Although you may start with a set idea for the trimming, you will probably need to adapt, or even change your mind, as you go along. Some tassels really hate ruffs, for example, or indeed anything around the neck at all, and the nice clean lines of the mold joining the skirt could be left undecorated.

I like plenty of movement in a tassel, particularly beaded ones, so I use things that hang and swing over the skirt. The practical side has to be considered too, as tassels get lots of handling. I would love to add a loose wire cage all around the head of a tassel, or wire curving out over the top of the skirt, but over time it would get squashed and distorted, so that idea has been put aside for further development.

What usually happens is that you finish a tassel on a Saturday evening and need to buy some large beads, or beads of a different shape, to finish the tassel off. If you live out in the country as I do, it may be impossible to shop for several days or even rely on efficient mail-order services, so you may decide to make something from the beads you do have—and use your imagination.

This chapter is full of ideas for trimmings made from small beads that give bulk, add weight, and decorate—all at the same time. I have suggested lots of variations and I'm sure that you will think of even more as you work.

As you plan your trimmings, keep the overall shape and proportions of your tassel in mind and ask yourself:

❖ Do I want the tassel to go in at the neck, or will the ruff hide the curve?

❖ Do I want the weight of the fringe to be at the bottom, or evenly distributed?

❖ Will adding braids (snailing) on the head make it too large for the skirt, which perhaps can be made longer by adding a central drop of yarn or beads?

❖ Should the weight be at the neck and the base of the skirt, or at only one spot?

Look at books of historical tassels for answers to such questions. If you can't decide, resort to the trial-and-error method. Even if you make extra trimmings that are wrong for the tassel in progress, they can always be put away, ready for that next tassel project.

RUFFS

Most tassels made from yarns have a ruff around the neck to hide any untidy construction that might show, and to serve as decoration. Beaded ruffs look even better and can be as simple as a string of larger beads, blackberries, or wired beads tied around the neck. The ruff can also be used at the top of the tassel head where the cord emerges.

Any of the braids given in this book can be used instead of a looped ruff, if you wish for a flatter result. They can be decorated with picots or massed loops on the edges, or have more beads sewn down the center of the strips. However, a looped beaded ruff made on a foundation strip of 2- or 4-bead peyote stitch is more like the yarn ruffs.

Method (narrow ruff)

Work a 2-bead strip just long enough to go around the neck of the tassel after you have added the skirt. There must be the same number of beads down each side of the strip.

Take a new thread and pass the needle through the first 2 beads of the strip. Pick up 5 beads and pass the needle back through the next 2 beads from the other side, making a loop over the top of the strip. Continue like this until the whole strip is covered.

Try the ruff around the neck to see if it is long enough, because adding the loops will have shortened it slightly. It should fit very tightly. If necessary, make the strip longer and add more loops. Hold the ruff around the neck and pass the needle through the 2 beads on the other end. Tie both ends of thread together, pull hard to tighten, and knot the threads.

The loops of beads can be made from larger seed beads, or a mixture of seed or cylinder beads and disks, tiny cubes, or triangles.

Tassels with beaded ruffs at the join of the neck and the head, or at the top of the skirt or all over the head.

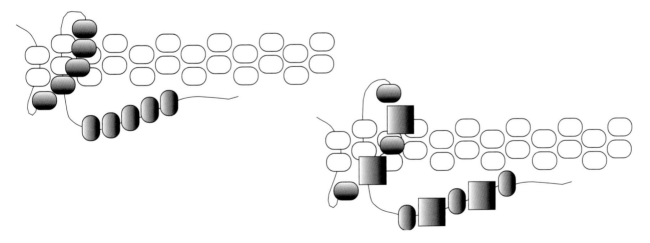

How to make a ruff on a 2-bead braid.

TRIANGLES

Beaded triangles can cover the top of a tassel skirt in the same way that knotted or buttonhole-stitched shapes do on many traditional tassels. Because brick stitch automatically decreases at the edges when it is worked flat, it is the best stitch to use for these triangles. A string of beads can hang from each point to reach down to the bottom of each skirt.

The triangles can be made in different sizes, but the instructions here are for the triangles used for the tassels in the photo opposite, where the loops at the top are gathered in to fit around the neck. I used cylinder beads, but seed beads are just as good, although the triangles will be slightly larger.

If you wish to make a longer shape, you can use bugles instead of beads, or try double brick stitch instead of single. If you wish to make a more truncated shape so that you can hang two strings of beads from the corners, just finish when you have come to the row with 3 or 5 beads on it.

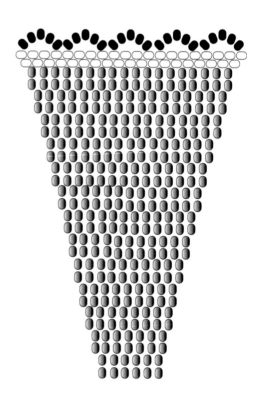

Making triangles with a looped edge to gather into the neck.

Materials
size 11 seed or cylinder beads

Method
Work a 2-bead peyote strip until there are 20 beads on one side and 19 on the other, leaving a long tail at the beginning. Work rows of flat brick stitch on the side with 19 beads, decreasing every row until there are only 2 beads left. Use method 2 for brick stitch so that no threads show on the outside edge of the triangle. Leave the thread hanging to hang beads from later. Using the beginning tail of the thread, work 5 loops of 5 or 7 beads each, according to the diagram. String beads from the point of each triangle to make a fringe, and finish off the thread.

Make two more triangles, Then take a doubled thread through the center bead of each loop on all three triangles. Tie the thread tightly around the neck of the tassel, pulling the loops in at an angle to the triangles so that they fall flat down over the yarn skirt of the tassel.

Two large tassels with overlapping triangles on the skirt (6½ and 8 inch), and a three-flower tassel with smaller overlapping triangles stitched to the cord.

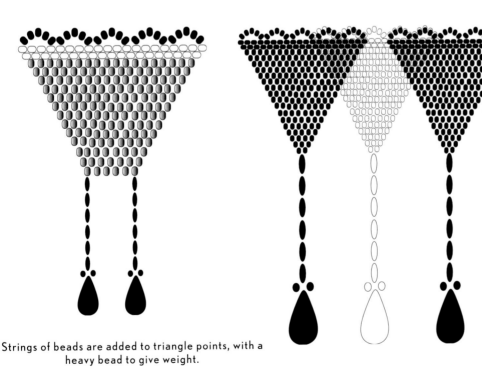

Strings of beads are added to triangle points, with a heavy bead to give weight.

THREE-FLOWER TASSEL

A slight variation on the triangles can turn them into flower petals, here attached to a tassel made at one end of a cord.

Materials

a cord, about 12 inches long or more
yarn for the tassel
size 11 seed beads

Method

Fold the cord in half and wrap the two cut ends firmly, using a cotton thread that grips well. Wrap yarn around a piece of card or wire frame. Cut it off at one side.

Lay the yarn on a table and the cord in the middle of the bundle, with the wrapped ends just left of the center point. Pick the bundle up, making sure that the yarn is evenly distributed around the cord, and wrap firmly around the whole bundle.

Pick up the loop of cord, allowing the yarn to fall down over the tassel. Distribute it evenly over the first wrapping, and wrap again just under the bulge, giving a smooth head and neck.

Beading: Work a 4-bead peyote strip until there are 15 beads on one side and 14 on the other, leaving a long tail at the beginning.

Work rows of flat brick stitch on the side with 14 beads, decreasing every row until there are only 2 beads left. Leave the thread hanging to hang beads from.

Using the beginning tail of the thread, work 5 loops of 3 beads each, according to the diagram. Work 2 more rows of 3-bead loops. Take the thread through the center bead of each loop on all three triangles.

Tie the thread tightly around the cord, pulling the loops in at an angle to the triangles so that they fall flat down

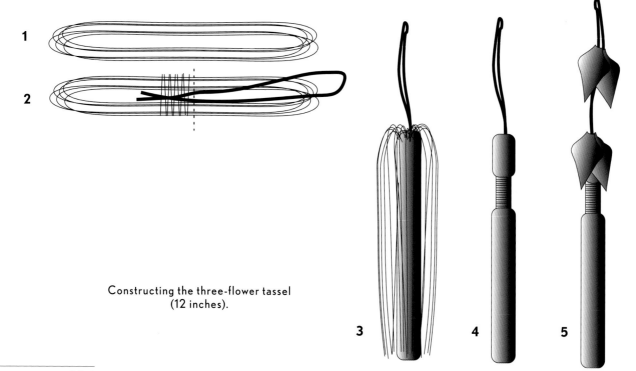

Constructing the three-flower tassel
(12 inches).

over the head of the tassel. Make two more petals and arrange them evenly around the cord, stitching them to it.

To form a collar, make a 4-bead peyote strip, wrap it around the cord, and "zip" it together. Finish off the ends of the thread by sewing them back and forth through the cord.

Make at least two more flowers of three petals each and sew them to the cord at intervals.

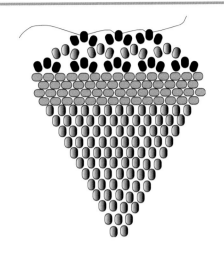

A smaller triangle for the three-flower tassel.

TINY CYLINDER BEADS

Beads made of beads are often the answer when you don't have any larger beads in your box and need a stronger accent in your cord, at the bottom of a fringe, or just to decorate a tassel head or neck.

Method 1 instructions are for the smallest size. They do not need anything inside them but are firm enough to keep their shape.

Method 2 is used for larger beads, made over small cylinders of wood, plastic, or metal. You can often find things around the house that you can cover: old bugle beads, children's plastic beads, bamboo tubes, or paper beads that you have made.

Method 1

Thread a needle with about 2 feet of thread. Pick up 6 beads and work flat peyote on them until there are 5 beads on each side. Zip the two edges together, fitting the up beads into the spaces on the other side, and taking the thread through each side alternately.

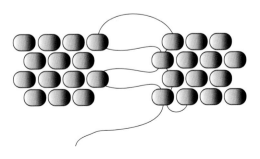

Simply "zip" the edges together.

Method 2

Pick up enough beads on the needle to match the length of the cylinder that you are covering. Work flat peyote for as many rows as you need to cover the cylinder. It should be a really tight fit, so stop a row or two before you think you need to.

Wrap the beading around the cylinder and zip it together, pulling the thread tight as you stitch it so that the edges meet.

Decorations: These tiny cylinder beads can have picots or a frill worked along the top and bottom edges, rows of extra beads sewn down or across them, or a netting worked over them. A small band can be sewn around the center of a bead, or the strip of peyote can be sewn around the center of a larger glass cylinder bead.

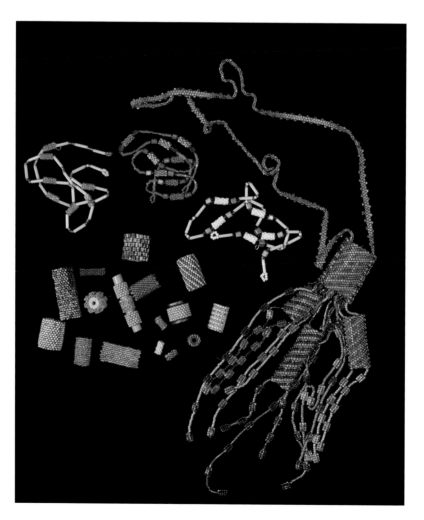

Tiny cylinder beads (method 1), flat beading wrapped around wooden or plastic cylinders to cover them, tiny cylinders incorporated into cords, and a bag with a fringe of beaded beads.

TINY FLOWERS

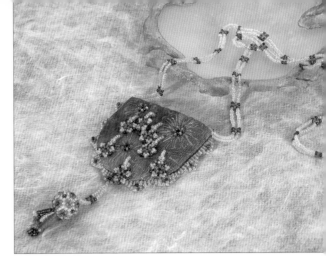

These tiny flowers can be used all around the neck of a tassel, can hang in strings from the neck over the skirt, or can be used to decorate a braided or netted tassel mold. They can be used flat, but I think they look better if a larger bead or small blackberry is sewn onto the center.

The flowers can be sewn back to back, perhaps with a bead between them to add bulk, or they can be piled up on top of each other, each one a different color.

Method 1

This method produces more of a flower shape. Here, two colors are used.

Thread 5 beads (color A), make a ring and go through the ring again, slipping through a couple of beads. Then, slip forward 1 bead at the end of every round following:

1st round. Add 1 bead (color A) through each bead.

2nd round. Add 2 beads (color B) through each bead. (10 beads)

3rd round. Add 1 bead (color A) through each bead.

4th round. Add 1 bead (color B) through each bead.

5th round. Go through 2 beads, add 2 beads (color B) through the next bead. Repeat to the end. (15 beads)

Method 2

Here, three colors are used. Thread 5 beads (color A), make a ring, and go through the ring again, slipping through a couple of beads. Then, slip forward 1 bead at the end of every round following:

1st round. Add 1 bead (color A) through each bead.

2nd round. Add 2 beads (color B) through each bead. (10 beads)

3rd round. Add 1 bead (color C) through the next bead, then 1 bead (color A)

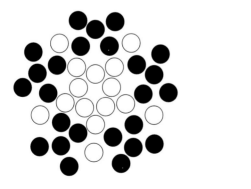
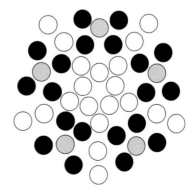

Tiny flowers patterns, method 1 and 2.

through the next bead. Repeat to end of round.

4th round. Add 1 bead (color B) through each bead.

5th round. Add 1 bead (color A) through the first bead, 2 beads (color B) through the next, then repeat to end. (15 beads)

6th round. Thread 1 bead (color A) through each bead.

7th round. Thread 1 bead (color A) through each bead.

8th round. Thread 1 bead (color A), 1 bead (color A), 1 bead (color B). Repeat to end of the round.

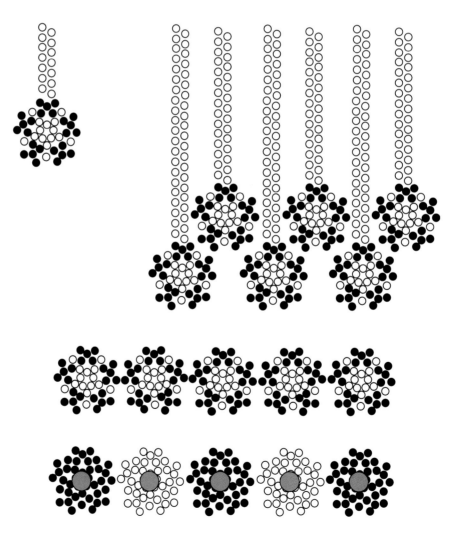

Tiny flowers can be used singly, in strips, or stitched back to back, hung on strings or braids, and used to decorate tassel necks or skirts.

BLACKBERRIES

These uneven little balls can hang from the bottom of fringes or can be threaded together to make a ruff around the neck of a tassel.

You will need about 25 (or more) size 11 seed or cylinder beads to make any sort of blackberry, so you can hide your not-so-nice beads in the center of them. If you are going to make more than one, you will need to count the number of beads each time to make sure they are the same size.

Method

Put a 15-inch length of thread through your needle and pick up 3 beads. Leaving a 5-inch tail, tie both ends together in a knot.

Pick up 1 bead and take the needle through the cluster of beads, not through a hole in a bead. Pick up another bead and take the needle through the cluster, back to the other side. Continue like this, picking up 1 bead at a time.

Roll the blackberry around in your

Blackberries on the black card, small cups, knots, and
tiny flowers for trimming tassels.

fingers as it gets bigger, to keep it in a nice shape. If there is a hollow, bring the needle up into the hollow and put a bead in it.

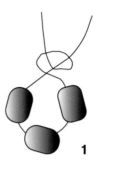
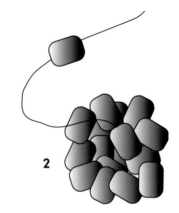

Repeatedly adding beads to a cluster makes a blackberry.

A tiny bag with blackberry fringe.

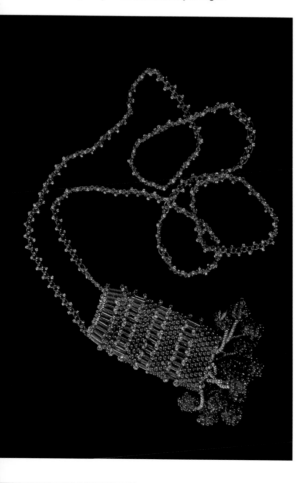

VARIATION

Try using different beads for the outside layer—perhaps triangles, or even cubes. If you use bugles, you will need to pick up 1 bugle and 1 bead, skip the bead, and go back through the bugle into the cluster.

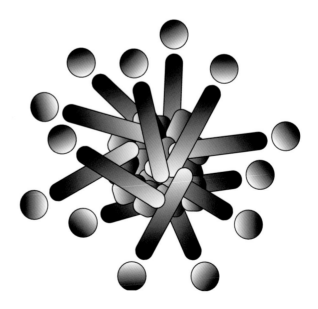

Adding bugle beads to make a spiny center.

These can be made in different sizes and piled inside each other, or stitched together back to back. You can sew a larger bead or small blackberry inside the cup. A string of them can make a ruff around the neck of a tassel, or they can hang informally down a string of beads on the skirt.

The cups look best when they are made using small beads, either cylinder beads or size 12 or 14 seed beads; they are rather crude-looking made with anything larger.

Method (small cup)

Thread 5 beads, make a ring, and go through the ring again, slipping forward through a couple of beads. Leave a 6-inch tail to sew the cup to the tassel. Then, slip forward 1 bead at the end of every following round.

1st round. Add 1 bead through each bead.

2nd round. Add 2 beads through each bead. (10 beads)

3rd, 4th, and 5th rounds. Thread 1 bead through each bead.

Finish the sewing thread off.

Method (larger cup)

Thread 5 beads, make a ring, and go through the ring again, slipping forward through a couple of beads. Leave a 6-inch tail to sew the cup to the tassel.

Slip forward 1 bead at the end of every following round.

1st round. Add 1 bead through each bead.

2nd round. Add 2 beads through each bead. (10 beads)

3rd round. Add 1 bead through each bead.

4th round. Add (1 bead in the first space and 2 beads in the next space). Repeat ( ) to end of the round. (15 beads)

5th, 6th, and 7th rounds. Add 1 bead in every space.

Finish the sewing thread off.

PATTERNS

Horizontal stripes: Change the color of the beads every 2 rows.

Spiral: Thread 5 beads in color a, make a ring and go through the ring again, slipping forward through a couple of beads. Leave a 6-inch tail to sew the cup to the tassel.

Then slip forward 1 bead at the end of every following round.

1st round. Add 1 color A bead through each bead.

2nd round. Add (1A and 1B) in the next space. Repeat ( ) until the end of the round.

3rd and 4th rounds. Add (1A in first space, 1B in next space). Repeat ( ).

5th, 6th and 7th rounds. Add 1A in the next space, 1B in the next, and 1A in the next. Repeat ( ).

Flower: This pattern uses 3 colors and gives a slightly wider shape. Thread 5 beads (color A), make a ring and go through the ring again, slipping through a couple of beads. Then slip forward 1 bead at the end of every following round.

1st round. Add 1 bead (color A) through each bead.

2nd round. Add 2 beads (color B) through each bead. (10 beads).

3rd round. Add 1 bead (color B) through the next bead, then 1 bead (color A) through the next bead. Repeat to end of the round.

4th round. Add 1 bead (color B) through each bead.

5th round. Add 1 bead (color A) through the first bead, 2 beads (color B) through next bead. Repeat to end. (15 beads)

6th round. Thread 1 bead (color A) through each bead.

7th round. Thread 1 bead (color A) through each bead.

8th round. Thread 1 bead (color A), 1 bead (color A), 1 bead (color B). Repeat to end of round.

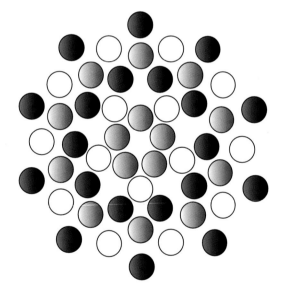

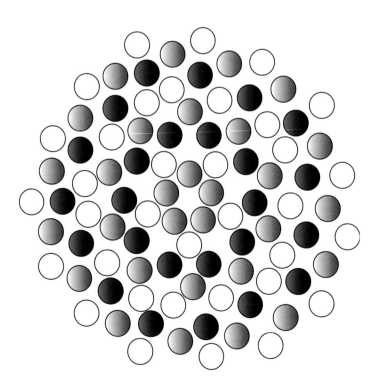

Making small and large cups (the small one fits inside the larger).

BLACK FLOWER TASSEL

This tassel with a flower-patterned netted skirt is added onto a painted mold and decorated with flat braids and small cups. There are two petticoats, which give a nice density to the skirt and show off the pattern. I used black cylinder beads for the two petticoats, and warm silver cylinder beads with gold and lavender small triangles for the flower pattern and the narrow braids. Large matching triangles are sewn to the center of the cups.

You will need to choose a very simple shape for the wooden mold, because the braids will not go in and out over a more complex one.

Start with the under petticoat and then add the middle one, and finally add the overskirt, in that order, so that you are always working on the top.

Materials

seed or cylinder beads, mainly one
    color but contrasting color for flower
    pattern larger beads, triangular or
    round, for flower centers
7 larger beads, for the centers of cups
    around the neck
a wooden tassel mold

Method

Thread enough beads on a very long thread to go around the neck of the tassel. The number of beads must be divisible by 4 so that you can hang the netting on it.

Take the thread through the beads again to make a ring and tie the ends tightly together.

Cord: Make two short fine cords and pull them through the mold, knotting them together at the base. Glue the knot in, pulling it up slightly into the hole.

Central drop: If you wish to include this, make four 2-bead peyote braids about 4 inches long, and sew them to the knot before you glue the cord in.

Under petticoat: Work 1 row of 5-bead netting into every fourth bead. Use a single color bead but, to make the netting easier, you could use a bead with a different texture as the spot bead.

Change to a 7-bead net and work until the skirt is long enough—two or three times as long as the mold.

Middle petticoat: Starting on the fifth row of the under petticoat, work 9-bead netting until it is as long as the under petticoat.

Overskirt: Work a 9-bead netting with a flower pattern into every fourth bead of the original string around the neck, following the chart pattern given on page 116. Use downer beads in between those that you used for the under petticoat.

Work 4 rows, and then change to an 11-bead net. Continue until the overskirt is the same length as the petticoats.

Braids: Work a 2-bead peyote braid—or any narrow flat braid—until it is long enough to go up the skirt, over the mold, through the cords and down the other side. Make another braid to match.

Sew the braids to the neck of the mold by threading through 2 beads of the braid, adding 7 or 8 beads, threading through 2 beads of the next braid, adding

Black flower tassel with clusters of small cups (5 inches).

7 or 8 beads, and so on until you come back to the beginning. Knot the ends of the thread tightly, pulling hard.

The 7 or 8 beads you have picked up act as "spacers"—to keep the braids in place, pulling the braid into the neck.

Decorate the braids with picots, using the small triangle beads in every fourth bead on each side.

Finishing the cord: Make a 2-bead peyote braid long enough to circle the cords tightly, and join them together. Pull the ring down the cord to the top of the mold and finish the thread off by sewing back and forth through the cord and the ring of beads.

Small cups on hanging braids: Make the small cups as given on page 113 and attach them to the base of the long braids, two to each braid. Sew a large bead into the center as you do this.

Add 3 or 4 more large triangles on each side of the braid, to look like flower buds.

Fringe: Add fringe to the points of both petticoats and the overskirt, following the diagram and using both sizes of triangle beads, with 4 seed or cylinder beads on each side.

Central drop: Decorate the bottom of each braid with 2 cups on each one and extra-large triangles, the same as the hanging braids.

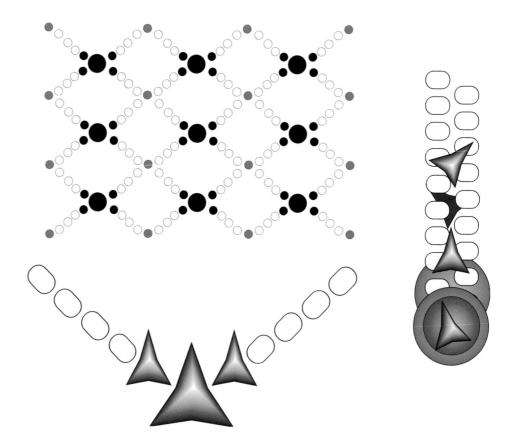

Flower pattern for the netted skirt, loop on the last row of netting, and narrow braid with cups and triangle beads.

CUBES AND SQUARES

Because so many shapes connected with beads and tassels are rounded, it is quite a relief to introduce some shapes with points and straight sides. Cubed beads, square pieces or dice from discarded games, and cubes or rectangles cut from wood or firm erasers can all be covered with peyote stitch, brick or square stitch, and used as tassel heads or to decorate skirts or fringes. However, by far the most convenient material to cover is thick card cut into ¼-inch or larger squares or rectangles. Thicker shapes or cubes can be made by gluing the squares or rectangles together. Triangles can be covered with brick stitch—make the triangle first and then cut the card to fit it.

The strips are a bit small for complex patterns, but you can use any of the color mixing patterns on page 16. When covered with beads the shapes are much larger, so make allowances for this.

PLAIN COVERING METHOD
Put an even number of beads on your needle to measure the width of the shape you are covering; a fraction larger is better than a fraction smaller.

Work an even number of peyote-stitch rows until the strip will go right around the beads when stretched out slightly. "Zip" the ends together. As you join the ends, pull the thread tightly. Then knot it.

Cover the narrow sides by threading the right number of beads to reach across the space and taking the needle up and down into the top row of beads on each side.

WEAVING METHOD
Larger pieces can be covered with narrow strips of beading, woven as they are added.

Work 2- or 4-bead strips of peyote or square stitch until the strip is slightly too long to go around the shape. Join it up and slide it onto the cube.

Work more strips and weave them through the first row (or rows) as you add them. The slack will be taken up by the weaving.

I don't bother to cover the corners, but you can if you wish by adding beads in the same way as the method above.

Cubes and square pieces of card covered with plain and woven beading, and a fringe using the beaded squares, twisted fringe, and spiral beading.

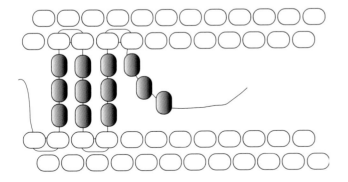

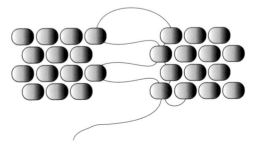

Joining beading to cover squares and cubes.

PAPER OR FABRIC BEADS

Rolled-up strips of paper or fabric make colorful and inexpensive beads which can be used as they are, covered with peyote beaded strips, or wrapped with colored wire.

They can be made on a knitting needle, a pencil if you wish to make one with a large hole for a tassel head, or on a bead maker.

Use any good-quality paper that can be colored or painted on, or use Christmas paper, brown wrapping paper, pages from magazines, or computer printouts.

Choose one of the shapes below, remembering that the length determines how fat the bead will be and the width of the strip how long it will be.

If you wish to make more than one bead the same size, you will need to enlarge the diagram to make a card template.

Method

Starting at the wide end, roll the paper firmly and evenly around the knitting needle. When you have rolled once or twice around the rod, spread glue down the center of the rest of the strip and finish rolling. Gently take it off the needle and let it dry.

If you are making a fabric bead, then you should use a fabric glue.

If you use a bead maker, life is much easier. Just slip the end of the paper strip in the slot of the rod and start rolling. Putting the glue on and rolling at the same time is a far speedier process, and you can make beads by the dozen.

DECORATIONS

These beads can be colored before or after they are made. Fabric beads can be painted with fabric paints and paper beads with any paint or varnish. The paint can be applied by dabbing, sponging, or any of the methods given in the first chapter, so that they match a wooden mold. Gold leaf makes a lovely finish.

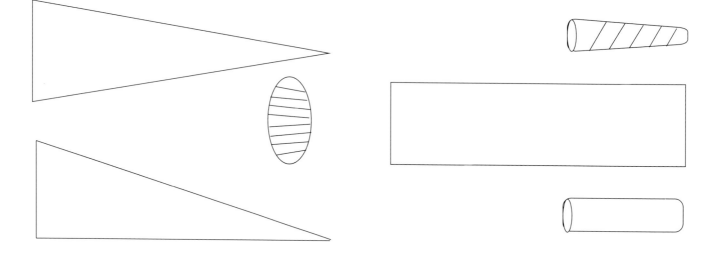

Paper shapes to make beads.

A copy of an Edwardian paper bead maker, paper beads painted and covered
with gold leaf, paper wrapped around pencils for Chinese tassels, and a fringe
of paper beads wrapped with wire and lengths of coiled wire.

ROLLED-PAPER TASSEL HEADS

Chinese tassel heads are often made from cylinders or ovals of rolled paper, and are wrapped with yarn.

You can make a version using a round pencil, a flat carpenter's pencil for an oval shape, or two hexagonal pencils held together with rubber bands. Press these last two gently to emphasize the oval shape.

Method

Cut a strip of fairly thick paper, something like sugar paper or wallpaper-lining paper, about 1 inch wide and 12 to13 inches long. Start rolling it around the pencil, then put glue right down the middle of the strip and continue rolling. Add more glue along the final edge. Allow to dry.

CHINESE TASSELS

These long, narrow tassels are made differently from most tassels, with half the skirt pulled through the central hole and allowed to fall down again around the outside of the tassel like a waterfall. Wrapping around the outside of the head secures it. These tassels are always long and elegant, without fullness.

While looking at the Chinese tassels in her collection, Lynn Horniblow worked out how to do this tassel. Some of the heads, even the flat oval ones, were made of wood, but many were made of rolled paper. My Chinese tassels are made in a different way, with the skirt tied on around the cord and falling over the rolled-paper head, to be wrapped around and secure all the yarn.

Once the tassel has been constructed, the head can be decorated with a beaded collar, using any of the braids given in this book, or with a netted bead covering. You could hang a beaded skirt from the collar, or bead the cord.

Chinese tassels made on rolled-paper beads with added beading.

Materials

rolled-paper tassel head

fine twisted cord about 10 inches long

yarn for the skirt

metallic or other contrasting fine thread for wrapping the head

skirt board, piece of card or a wire frame, minimum 12 inches long (To make it really elegant, I prefer a length of about 18 or 20 inches.)

beads to decorate the head

Method

Make the basic tassel, using a rolled-paper cylinder according to method 3 on page 22.

Wrap the tassel with metallic thread, or a yarn of the same or contrasting color.

Netted head: Make a cylinder of vertical netting following the instructions on page 78. Slip it over the wrapped head, and pull it in fairly tightly at the top of the head.

Thread a new thread through the spot beads at the bottom of the netting, adding 2 or 3 beads between each one. Pull the thread tightly so that the netting is a bit tight just under the rolled-paper head. Take the thread right through the whole ring again and finish it off.

Finishing: Comb the skirt, then steam and trim the bottom ends.

Braid collar: Make a bead braid using any of the braids given earlier to fit tightly around the thread-wrapped head.

Wrap the beading around the head and zip it together fitting beads into spaces on the opposite side. Stitch through beads alternately from each side, pull the ends tight and tie into a firm knot.

You can make one wider ring, perhaps with a narrow ring over it, or make two narrow ones.

FOUR-TASSEL VARIATION

Wrap the rolled-paper head with a fine cotton yarn, using a needle and a very long thread—about 4 yards if you feel you can handle that long a length, and doubled if it is very fine. To start, hold the tail of the head firmly against the paper roll and drop the needle down inside the roll. Continue wrapping the yarn neatly around and around the roll. Finish the yarn off by tying it to the beginning tail.

Wrap the yarn around the skirt board, add a cord, and pull the hank through the hole as given in the instructions above. Make bead collar to fit over the paper head, and four small ones for the extra tassels.

Divide the yarn at the top of the tassel into four equal sections. Wrap each one with a smaller collar. Finish off the bead thread on each small tassel by sewing it into the bottom of the main tassel and back into the small tassel to secure them.

The top is finished off with a gold ring and a yarn-wrapped wooden bead.

WIRE BEADS

There are so many beautifully colored wires available now that it is very tempting to use them to make beads which can be as large as you like and smooth or textured. They can be used at the base of a fringe or around the neck of a tassel, simulating a ruff. Tiny ones can be stitched all over a tassel head, or long lengths of coiled wire can be made into loops that hang down over the tassel skirt.

Wired beads can be made on a paper bead maker, a coiling gizmo, a mattress needle, or a fine knitting needle. The coiling gizmo is faster, but the beads look much the same however you make them. A friend of mine, Ian Lever, made the gadget in the photograph, which I can also use for rolling tassel molds.

Method 1 (coiled-wire beads)

Use wire about 20 or 24 gauge so that these beads will have enough body to keep their shape.

Bend about 1/4 inch of the cut end of

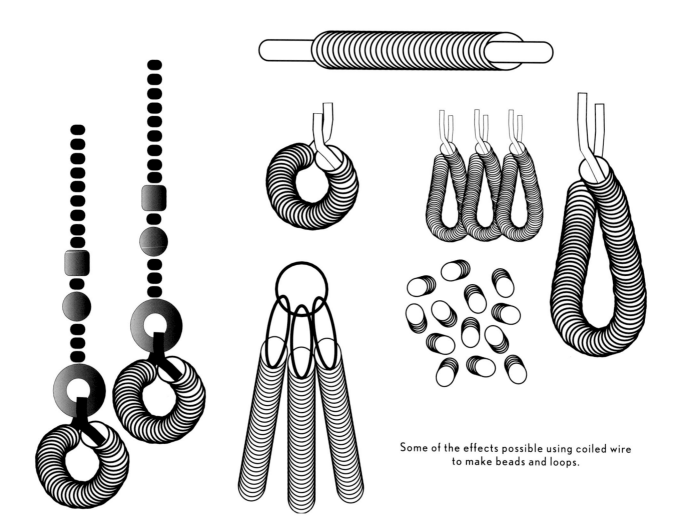

Some of the effects possible using coiled wire
to make beads and loops.

the wire and insert it into the slot in the bead maker rod or the chuck of the coiling gizmo. You do not need to do this if you are using a needle. Then coil the wire a set number of times around the rod or needle and cut the end.

Slide the bead off the rod. Bend the ends of the wire into the holes at each end of the bead, to hide them.

For a more complex bead, coil a longer length, about 3 inches or even longer if you wish, and thread an 8-inch length of wire through the hole. Wind the end of this threaded wire onto the rod or needle and make two or three turns. Then, working slowly and carefully, wind the coiled wire around the rod, making sure that it does not slip along the threaded wire. Finish with a few turns of the threaded wire.

Method 2 (wrapped-wire beads)

You will need a wire that will go through the holes of your beads. Try gauge 28, which should go through seed or cylinder beads.

Thread about 30 beads onto the end of the wire, leaving the other end attached to the reel.

Wind about 15 coils of plain wire around the rod or needle as a base for the bead.

Wind more wire irregularly back over this base, pushing up a bead about

every quarter or half turn. Wind from side to side, pushing a bead up every time you see a space.

Finish off by wrapping plain wire over the whole bead so that it looks like a cage. Bend the cut ends of the wire into the holes.

There is no end to the variations that you can do using one or another of these methods; some of them are illustrated in the drawing opposite. I am especially fond of the wire-wrapped-over-painted-paper beads (made on the bead maker), some of which have been made using my computer printouts. Wire can also be wrapped over thin polyethylene tubing, which gives it bulk without weight. The tubing can be painted beforehand if you prefer, or covered with gold leaf.

A wire-coiling gizmo, some coiled wire beads and tassel decorations, and a tassel and tiny bag using wrapped wire beads.

SPIRAL BEADING

This method, a cross between peyote stitch and netting, simulates the hanging spirals of fine metal wire that you often see on the skirts of magnificent historical tassels in great houses or museums.

Some people can work these in their hands. I find it easier to use a support, either a wooden skewer or very fine bamboo knitting needle. Anything larger gives a spiral that is too big for most tassels.

To start, just use seed beads until you get the hang of the method. The nicest spirals, however, use combinations of beads and can include bugles, triangles, cubes, and larger round beads.

Keeping a tight tension all the time is crucial, especially when using bugles or larger beads; otherwise, the whole thing will flop all over the place. Hold the thread against the support with your thumb between every stitch and, every so often, pull the whole ring tighter.

Method

Thread a bead in color A, then 3 beads in color B. Repeat this combination 3 or 4 times, until the entire length will fit around the skewer. See diagram 1 on page 125. There should be a slight gap between the first and last beads; otherwise, the spiral will become too loose.

Take the needle through the first color A bead; wind the tail around the top of the skewer and secure it with an elastic band. Do not knot the thread as you would in previous methods.

Pick up 1 bead in color A, then 3 beads in color B and take the needle through the second bead A of the previous row. Pull the thread tight.

Continue like this for the length of the spiral, measuring it against the tassel skirt. Make it slightly shorter than the skirt because it might drop a bit after it is finished.

Samples of spiral beading for use on fringes and over tassel skirts.

VARIATIONS

❖ Use 3 small beads and 1 large one. Repeat. (Diagram 2)

❖ Use 1 small bead, 1 medium, 1 small and 1 large bead. Repeat. (Diagram 3)

❖ Use 1 bugle and 1 small bead. Repeat. (Diagram 4)

❖ Use 1 bugle, 1 small and 1 medium bead. Repeat. (Diagram 5)

Always take the stitch through the largest bead; otherwise, the rows will pile up on each other.

DECORATIONS

These spirals can be decorated with rows of picots following a spiral line of beads, or have short lengths or loops of strung beads hanging from them.

One spiral can make a single tassel, with a hank of thread pulled through it, or clusters of short spirals can be worn as earrings. A spiral can be worked around a cord to wear as a necklace.

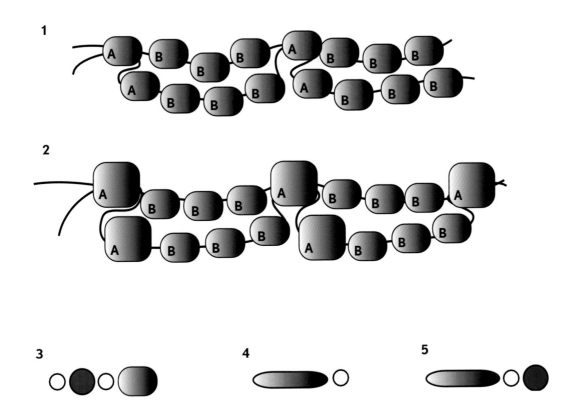

Basic method and variation patterns for spiral beading.

INDEX